N.RHODES

Sant

The Santiago Calatrava exhibition in the RIBA Florence Hall, 1992. Photograph: Geremy Butler.

Santiago Calatrava

Edited by Dennis Sharp

E & FN SPON

An Imprint of Chapman & Hall

London · Glasgow · Weinheim · New York · Tokyo · Melbourne · Madras

Second Edition
Published in association with Book Art

Published by E & FN Spon, an imprint of Chapman & Hall, 2–6 Boundary Row, London SE1 8HN, UK

Chapman & Hall, 2–6 Boundary Row, London SE1 8HN, UK

Blackie Academic & Professional, Wester Cleddens Road, Bishopbriggs, Glasgow G64 2NZ, UK

Chapman & Hall GmbH, Pappelallee 3, 69469 Weinheim, Germany

Chapman & Hall Inc., One Penn Plaza, 41st Floor, New York, NY 10119, USA

Chapman & Hall Japan, Thomson Publishing Japan, Hirakawacho Nemoto Building, 6F, 1-7-11 Hirakawa-cho, Chiyoda-ku, Tokyo 102, Japan

Chapman & Hall Australia, Thomas Nelson Australia, 102 Dodds Street, South Melbourne, Victoria 3205, Australia

Chapman & Hall India, R. Seshadri, 32 Second Main Road, CIT East, Madras 600 035, India

First edition 1992 by Book Art

Second edition 1994 by E & FN Spon, in association with Book Art

© 1992, 1994 Book Art/Calatrava Valls SA

Typeset by Fox Design, Bramley, UK
Printed in Great Britain by St Edmundsbury Press, Bury St Edmunds, Suffolk

ISBN 0 419 19570 X

Most of the illustrations have been supplied by Calatrava Valls SA, Zürich who, with the editors, gratefully acknowledge the work of the following photographers:
Paolo Rosselli, Milan
Heinrich Helfenstein, Zürich
Waltraud Krase
Ege Photography, Lucerne
Other photographers are mentioned in the text.

Illustrations on pp. 80 (1–3), 81 (4), 82 (1–3) and 83 (5) are reproduced with permission from *El Croquis 57, Santiago Calatrava 1990/1992*, El Croquis Editorial, Madrid; the illustration on p. 61 (5) is reproduced with permission from *Santiago Calatrava 1983/93, Catalogo de la exposición antologica en la Lonja de Valencia*, El Croquis Editorial, Madrid.

Edited by Dennis Sharp

Assisted by Anthony Tischhauser and Yasmin Shariff

Editorial assistance in London by Catherine Slessor

Design by Malcolm Frost

Stadelhofen Station, Zürich

Contents

The Bird, Sculpture, 1986

Preface

Santiago Calatrava, the Spanish-born architect and engineer, enjoys a worldwide reputation. His elegant bridge designs, spectacular airport buildings and museum and concert hall projects place him in the forefront of recent architectural developments in Europe. Eschewing the stylistic overtones of recent architectural fashions Calatrava's work is unique. His creations are frequently referred to as beautiful structures, a term hardly applied to any other architects' work since Frank Lloyd Wright. During the decade or so since he set up practice in Switzerland in 1981 he has taken up the challenge of reviving a design tradition that lays emphasis on the production of exciting, dynamic structural forms and new means of aesthetic expression. He claims 'there is a certain exercise in engineering aesthetics to be undertaken in the design of a bridge and I feel that the integration of technology and aesthetics deserve special attention'. The attention he refers to may be compared to that of the work procedures of the old 'Master Builder'. Like his creative predecessors (and Gaudí might be used as one example) he draws everything out at conception, slowly elaborating ideas into sketch working or shop drawings and calculations before producing scale models which suggest the final forms of a project.

It was this process that came through so clearly at the time of the hugely successful exhibition of Calatrava's work held at the RIBA in London in 1992, under the auspices of the Generalitat Valenciana, Spain. It is also the theme of this survey of his work. The first edition of this book served as a fully illustrated catalogue for the London exhibition but it soon sold out. Its re-publication therefore in a revised and expanded second edition is most welcome. It has allowed for the addition of a number of new projects at the time of a further London exhibition, at the Bruton Street Gallery in Mayfair as part of the Spanish Arts Festival, Spring, 1994.

The recent projects that have been incorporated in this new edition and shown in the exhibition include the elaboration of the project for a 'Bioshelter' at the Cathedral of St. John the Divine in New York, the development of the premiated design for the renovation of the German Reichstag, Berlin, the modular station designs for London Underground plc, recent work for the new Science Centre, Valencia and the new Trinity Bridge for the City of Salford.

The Salford bridge, which provides a pedestrian link to the heart of Manchester's business district, will be the first project of Calatrava's to be built in Britain. It is due for completion at the end of 1994. It is still hoped that an earlier scheme for the East London River Crossing might be revived. It was originally intended for the developer Stanhope, but rejected by the Ministry of Transport. During the period of the RIBA Exhibition a vast number of people, recognising the inherent beauty and significance of the new bridge as a gateway to London, signed a petition demanding that it be reconsidered by the Minister. That is still the aim two years later.

The close involvement of the Calatrava office was an essential ingredient in the preparation of this book and the exhibitions. Without the fastidious, scholarly and generous cooperation of Anthony Tischhauser, from Zürich, this book would never have materialized. Its first edition was supported by the Generalitat Valenciana and the British Cement Association. BCA's continuing interest in the publication, and in Calatrava's work generally, is gratefully acknowledged. Special thanks are also extended to Catherine Slessor for help with the texts, to Sr F. Serrano Súner y Polo, for his enthusiastic support, and to DSA staff and students who, far beyond the call of business and study, have contributed to both publications and exhibitions. Finally, my thanks must go to Santiago and Tina Calatrava, without whom none of this would have been possible, or worthwhile.

Dennis Sharp

Santiago Calatrava: Building Cultural Bridges

Dennis Sharp

Wir müssen ständig den Weg suchen,
bei dem die Wahrheit nicht leidet
und das Gefühl nicht hungert.
Bruno Taut

Portrait by Heinrich Helfenstein.

If there was any need to prove that we had entered a new architectural age then the work of Santiago Calatrava would definitely be used to support the case. His work is unique, a distinct product of these times. It is original and strongly inventive, individualistic, innovative and, in the way it challenges traditional architectural and engineering ideas, thoroughly relevant. Calatrava brings together engineering and architecture in projects that pursue beauty and harmony as a goal. 'I am interested in new goals that are partly the product of analysis and partly intuition', he said in an RIBA lecture in 1990. Immensely accomplished from a technical viewpoint his work has also been described as idealistic and highly personal. James Sutherland has called him a 'one man orchestra'!

In presenting Calatrava's work as something new and original it is necessary to be more specific than these generalisations might suggest. We have to ask, what is it about Calatrava's work that demands our attention? Where do the roots of this phenomenon lie? Does it need to be categorised to make its contemporary relevance and uniqueness clearer? Or, can the work stand on its own as a new direction in architecture? Currently two aspects of Calatrava's work seem to dominate: his rhythmically designed and well balanced bridges and a series of evocative and dynamic new buildings. The former have become so numerous during his brief ten years of active practice there is no longer any need to identify them individually. Their characteristic appearance underlines a way of designing if not a specific style. Calatrava has raised bridge design to an art form. 'Bridge building in my view', he has said, 'is the most architectural role of the engineer, especially as bridges form such an important point of reference in a town and can be used to add excitement to a dull landscape.'

It is possible to refer to a bridge by Calatrava nowadays and people will begin to nod knowingly as they used to when Robert Maillart's name was mentioned. It is a remarkable achievement for a relatively young architect and engineer to have such a high international public profile. For him bridge design has become an important technical, aesthetic and urban challenge, as well as a key to so many other environmental issues. In a sense all of Calatrava's buildings are 'bridges', although some span cultural divides rather than structural ones. While it is well known that Calatrava does not like to elaborate at any length on his intentions and his written descriptions are rather perfunctory, when offered they do contain many layers of thought which relate to wide cultural matters as well as aesthetic ones. His sculptures in particular, which have been cautiously developed from his analytical and statical studies, might well be described as scientific summaries of his aesthetic views. Indeed here is the bridge passage between art and technology. Calatrava, unlike Nervi, has never committed himself to a specific aesthetic attitude or theory nor divulged at any length the methodologies behind his creative processes. As one of his chief mentors, Felix Candela, has written: 'For what Santiago Calatrava sets out to create, and actually does create, are real works of art, even when he is dealing with the most prosaic of problems.' And again, with typical shrewdness,

Candela goes on to say that he is able '...to tackle the most complicated problems with clearly defined aesthetic aims and to come up with enviably elegant and surprisingly simple solutions...that simplicity, delight and cheerfulness in appearance that Michelangelo regarded as the essence of a true work of art.'

Originally Calatrava was trained as an architect at the Escuela Technica Superior de Arquitectura de Valencia, Spain, the city near which he was born in July 1951. He graduated in 1973. Soon afterwards the gradual metamorphosis began of the architect into the joint civil engineer. In 1975 he commenced a course of study in civil engineering at the Eidgenössische Technische Hochschule (ETH), Zürich. After finishing his graduate course he went on to complete a post-graduate PhD thesis in the ETH's Architecture Department on 'Zur Faltbarkeit von Fachwerken' ('On the foldability of space frames'), a subject he often returns to. In 1981 he set up an independent architecture and civil engineering office in Zürich. Today he has offices in Paris and Valencia as well.

A new age
The new age I referred to at the outset was that of the current post industrial era and the entry into a new internationalist phase which was so clearly prophesized by people such as the late R. Buckminster Fuller and Marshall McLuhan. They had predicted the new reality of a media-based 'Global Village' which, among other things, has recently ushered in the universal designer. Calatrava's practice has largely been sustained, if not exactly generated, by international competition

successes, and by prestigious foreign commissions. The subsequent establishment of his worldwide reputation has been supported by the ubiquitous international technical press. There has been a constant process of acceleration which has kept him on the move, another condition of the global consultant. In Calatrava's case there has been little need to fabricate or hype up publicity as his talent and design skills have proved constant. His originality has been as genuine and regular as a

neap tide. What has emerged, however, in the widespread publicity that Calatrava's work has enjoyed is the simplicity and directness of his means of communication and, consequently, a minor revolution in presentational and graphical techniques. Some of Calatrava's means of communicating his architectural ideas appear rather traditional, and central to all his presentations (particularly for the many competitions he enters and usually wins) are the use of scale models and freehand drawings

through which the elements of his schemes are portrayed.

The art of seeing

Until quite recently he has studiously eschewed computer technology in developing the design aspects of his projects. He has chosen – and it is not uncommon with other architects working in Switzerland – to stick with orthodox drawing techniques using computers in the Zürich office largely for calculation purposes. But with a significant build-up of work recently his Paris office has now moved into the field of computer aided design. However, for Calatrava the importance of sketching cannot be underestimated. It is his way of seeing or 'seeing through drawing', to use a phrase coined by Philip Rawson a few years ago for his BBC series on drawing techniques. Drawing accurately is an ability afforded to very few people, although fundamental to most artistic endeavour. But frequently – in both architecture and engineering conceptualisation – those who can draw well cannot always translate their ideas into a new reality. Others, like Antoni Gaudí, Erich Mendelsohn, Le Corbusier and now Calatrava himself, clearly can and have.

Shapes are made out of marks; planar forms can suggest three-dimensional reality. In Calatrava's work buildings and bridges flow from the marks on paper that summarily outline profound spatial, aesthetic and structural inventions. That they are frequently so simply stated and so clear in functional and symbolical intentions is often the result of the clarity of the initial concept and drawings. Obviously they can be compared to the

1
Calatrava's early pencil sketch of Le Corbusier's Church Notre Dame de Ronchamps.

2
One of Calatrava's life studies – a detail from a page in an undated sketchbook.

3
Stadelhofen Railway Station, Zürich, loggia detail, 1983–90.

4
A drawing for the Spandau Railway Station project, Berlin, which has overtones of Mendelsohn's Expressionist sketches n.d.

5
Skeleton of a dog.

sketches of Erich Mendelsohn. However, one should not be too quickly tempted to draw the conclusion that they form part of a greater corpus of Expressionistic architecture, even though at times they bear a strong resemblance to the productions of that period in the 1920s. But each sketch idea has to be built upon. It has to develop and mature. In Calatrava's case this takes time and endless variations: often large amounts of time. More recently, with so many projects in the design stages or under construction at any time, the development process has had to be accelerated and checked by the aid of computers. This is not something that Calatrava, whose conceptualising hitherto has not been exactly computer friendly, would allow to interfere with the consecutive flow of a design solution. Increasingly in the Paris office computers are playing a more significant role than that of calculators. But as in Behnisch's or Erskine's recent work the computer's place and role is still largely at the production, specification development, managerial and statical end and much less used at the formative creative edge. Like these architects Calatrava uses the well established techniques of revising, redrawing and colouring as the sketched-out ideas develop, as well as making models at various scales.

3

The London exhibition aimed to explore these processes and to display a number of the scale models that Calatrava had constructed over the last few years in collaboration with his Zürich-based model maker. Zabarowski is a master craftsman who deals with architectural models as if they were Swiss-made precision instruments.

4

They become the tools that derive from and follow through the gestation and development of Calatrava's own design ideas. This mutual respect and creative interaction between the two parties has produced some of the most evocative and telling architectural models seen over the last few years. Many of them have been carefully photographed by the talented Zürich photographer Heinrich Helfenstein. Calatrava's recent preoccupations with model making has also allowed him to explore further his interest in the movability of structural frames.

Natural forms and material
The relationships Calatrava sets up in his designs, and the quality of his structural inventions – which combine order with expression – distinguish his work from that of many other designers working today. He draws on a bewildering variety of inspirational sources and impulses, the most dominant of which is the growth and form of the world of nature. However, unlike the Art Nouveauistes of the turn of the century period, with whom his work is often compared, he does not draw upon nature as a source or repository of

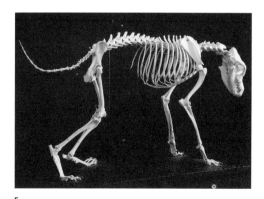

5

Dennis Sharp

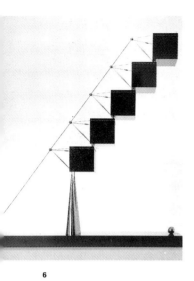

6

forms nor as a resource for decorative ideas. Nature provides a stimulus for the creative process. He can therefore be seen to be more in line with the interpretative approach of Antoni Gaudí rather than with, say, Guimard, Van de Velde, Horta or even the young Peter Behrens, whose interests were more naturalistic and often purely plagiaristic.

Nature is dominated by a dynamically balanced symmetry (or near symmetry); so is Calatrava's work. In nature structure is clearly expressed; so it is in Calatrava's work. But as it is employed in a subtle way and is not in imitation (or even a translation of formal contexts) it becomes more ubiquitous and exciting. References to nature can be found everywhere in Calatrava's work, in the numerous sketches (from the pure life study to the evocative sketch of a natural setting) right through to the built forms. Having eschewed imitation, however, its role is not so easily defined in say the way that Frank Lloyd Wright's 'universal' organic architecture is. It is much more specific to each project. The outward form may well exhibit organic analogies with nature, but it is the inner creative process that establishes its expression. Site characteristics do indeed dominate in the Wrightian sense in Calatrava's work, but it is the nature of the material that really establishes the nature of the form, to paraphrase Eliel Saarinen.

The many drawings to be found in his sketchbooks (and indeed on any scrap of paper that may have come his way) confirm a relentless search and curiosity about the expressive potentiality and nature of things. Often the

drawing of an object turns into a telling, simplified and symbolic device which becomes memorable at the artistic level, like the sketch of a flying bird or the skeleton of a dog (a model of which, incidently, is often shown in Calatrava exhibitions). These diagrams become thought-provoking metaphors that can be seen to be translated into structural terms in recent projects for Lyon and Bilbao. Whilst these exercises are seldom translated directly into built forms they play their residual and inspirational role in the process that leads up to the final project. The final result is often seen translated into the most original in situ or pre-cast concrete forms or welded steel elements. The Stadelhofen Railway Station in Zürich, which incorporates a dramatically side-lit, almost Piranesian pedestrian undercroft (now ruined by the traducing effects of accumulated commercial pressures which have systematically destroyed the visual clarity of this subterranean space) indicates the degree of amalgamation of materials and forms that can occur in one of Calatrava's more complex projects. And in all this the functional element is never lost. Stadelhofen, a busy interchange at any time, is well liked by the people who use it. In a greater urban context the station is superbly integrated and has helped to create a place redolent with appropriate references (some indeed very poetic, like the hanging gardens and the portcullis doorway to the undercroft) to its uses and circulation routes. An elegant staircase rises from one end of a platform on a cantilevered steel tube support that winds its way up to the upper floor's open pergola which one day will be encapsulated in the green shrubbery which it was designed to receive. This

6
Many of Calatrava's sculptures are concerned with relationships between three-dimensional objects, balance and gravitational pull. Running torso, 1985. Chrome plated steel.

7
Sketch of the staircase at the Tabourettli Theatre, Basle.

8
Spitalfields Gallery, London 1991 (Project).

Dennis Sharp

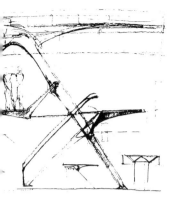

7

8

is an architecture with a built-in dimension of history, adaptation and a change – a *Gesamtkunstwerk*, in the broadest possible meaning of that much overworked term. To some people today laboriously drawing and sketching out a scheme may well appear an old fashioned, even ingenuous way of working. For me least it underlines another point. Santiago Calatrava designs within that continuity of Continental traditions in which 'the eye rules the mind'. As Gombrich and others have been at pains to state this is one of the unique contributions an artist can make to culture. It is, of course, part of the Renaissance tradition of the architect seeking to order and control the visible universe. The depiction of this world would be achieved by graphic representation. There are many similarities in the way Calatrava works – particularly with the desire to create an identifiable and harmonious whole with the Masters of the *Cinquecento*. But this analogy must not go too far, it would be too glib to speak of him as a new *Homo Universale* when what we are observing is the emergence of a completely different breed – the New European.

New European man
This is not simply flattery. Santiago Calatrava is patently a pan-European. He converses in many European languages having learnt, after his mother tongue, French in a period in Paris as a youth, German at Zürich, English by necessity and Italian by desire. He also speaks Swedish. The new European image comes from the fact that he has worked right across Europe. He spends many hours of his working life in aeroplanes exercising his responsibilities in site supervision, job visits

and public appearances in many countries. His desire to maintain his main office in neutral (and independent?) Switzerland is perhaps fortuitous with, until now, few commissions coming from that country – with the notable exception of the important Stadelhofen Railway Station in Zürich. His sojourn there can surely be read as symbolic and expedient. A Spaniard in the craft workshop of Europe, he has a remarkably loyal and committed staff there and Zürich is about the right size for a comfortable, culturally aware and internationally minded community. Here in London, Calatrava's major exhibition in 1992 formed part of the RIBA Architecture Centre's cultural programme, with its emphasis on internationalism, materials and creativity. It was made possible by a generous grant from the Generalitat Valenciana and was designed to show as wide a range of Calatrava's work as possible. It indicated through many examples the way his various drawing, painting and model making techniques and his creative methods come together in a survey of recent bridges and buildings. Additionally, there were a number of recent sculptures on display. The emphasis of the exhibition was perhaps not so far reaching and comprehensive as the previous year's large retrospective exhibition in Zürich, which incidently, like the RIBA, had attracted more visitors to the venue than any previous show on architecture. But comprehensiveness had not been the aim in London. Celebration might be a better word. It celebrated the erection of many bridges: between art and science, people and buildings, old materials and new forms, as well as Calatrava and an entirely new, and appreciative audience.

Dennis Sharp

1
Lucerne, postcard view of the new
railway station around 1900.
Photograph: Werk-archithèse.

2
Lucerne, aerial view from the North,
1991. Photograph: Werk, Bauen and
Wohnen.

1

2

Santiago Calatrava and the Nebulous City

Bernhard Klein

Lucerne, 5.2.71: the flames rage and roar through the entrance hall to the railway station. The city, a destination on a stage of the modern Grand Tour like Avenches in the 18th century, is suddenly robbed of its gateway to the world. Not, however, the world of one of its seven wonders. Paul Valéry would certainly only have counted this amongst buildings happy enough to have a voice, and nothing more[1]. For 75 years the silhouette of this giant dome had ruled supreme, with only the great backdrop of the Alps to dwarf it (1). If, 200 years ago in Avenches, you had visited the Roman ruins of Helvetia's capital in the hope of being over-whelmed by an impression of some expired greatness, then, in the same way, the modern Lucerne will lure you with its newborn 'trifles'[2]. Coincidence saved the station portal, a kind of Triumphal Arch, from the fury of those flames and, transposed, coincidence now helps round off the decorative hotchpotch of architectural trivialities which we see today – but not, as if to reassure, without first having cast a cocky sideways glance towards the Parisian Arc du Carousel[3]. Cocky, because it is known that it was through this kind of gateway the defeated armies of ancient times

were forced to march, through which the travellers of the 19th century were ushered, and then, in the project phase, through which now only air should be ducted, air extracted from the 'sensitively located' underground car park beneath. These rescued stones had lost the power of speech. They had been struck dumb. But – and this was well worth a sideways glance from the conservationists and the politicians, not of course forgetting the planners – this 'sort of historical' monument attracts the observer's attention, acts as if it must be central within the expanse of station square and lake (2): an urban architecture, distantly reminiscent of Camillo Sitte (1843–1903) and reminiscent, too, of the 'old Kaiser era' with its already decaying strictly hierarchical social structure. Calatrava doesn't even enter into this kind of questionable centripetality; his 1983-designed entrance hall for the new station building by Lucerne architects Hans-Peter Ammann and Peter Baumann is indeed totally classicistic in its layout. Yet the 16 F-shaped concrete supports, which in front are supported by slender steel columns and from which the glass roof construction is suspended,

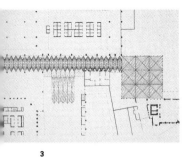

3

4

form regularly spaced rows along a length of 109 metres. Façade, space and constructional principle should (according to Calatrava) fuse together into a transparency[4]. The station portico is not conceived as the eye of a needle between inner city and outer city, through which travellers must thread their way. It should rather be seen as the penetrating zone of a conversation between inner and outer. This conception, deliberately applied in Zürich-Stadelhofen, forced not only the traditionalised urban planners in Lucerne, but also those in Zürich, to stand on their heads, depriving them of their historically unfounded 'trifles'. Santiago Calatrava: is he really a theme for urban planning historians? The Lucerne portico marks the commencement of a new code, during the course of which the alternating relationship centre, periphery and surrounding countryside assumes architectonic form. It has become the basis of a monumentality which is Calatrava's own. In the consciousness of the awful experience of the first half of the 20th century, it is of burning interest, and can be quickly disregarded as being a 'Station Square–Triumphal Arch' type of architecture, deemed relevant to the history of urban planning.

II

Nowadays, it need no longer be explained that the history of urban planning does not actually end with the 'Baroque' eve of the French revolution. Nor that something appears along with Ildefonso Cerda (1815–76), Arturo Soria y Mata (1844–1920) or Ebenezer Howard (1850–1928) that we now, out of embarrassment, name 'City'. We consider only fleetingly the actual meaning of that turn of

phrase, 'to go into the city'. An inside and an outside to a city had already ceased to exist 200 years ago[5]. We find ourselves in the midst of a change of mentality, a change from *City* to *Nebulous City*[6].

If we occupy ourselves with a loosely traditional history or urban planning up to the present time, a history actually serving only as a boundary between past and future, then another question arises, namely: how does Calatrava approach the historically loaded theme of *City/Nebulous City*? How does Calatrava face this change in mentality? A position, clear from the outset, which opposes the core of the city with its 'preserved' remoteness in relation to the periphery and surrounding landscape, is not detectable. A whole series of projects can be included in this tradition, which has been characterised in the Ancien régime as Embellissement, containing both the sublime and the political: I mean those galleries in London and Toronto (3), those bridges in Barcelona (4) and Merida, or that science museum in Valencia (5). These buildings and projects correct an underdeveloped or failed social space by the architectonic means of real or virtual connection. Calatrava's corrections are not in context. They are not stitched together as a result of an analysis of either buildings or the site to be developed, in accordance with the historical aspects as practised earlier by the imitators of the neo-rationalistic school of the seventies and eighties, and who in so doing suffocated the dynamic development of the site. Rather, Calatrava's architectonic interventions take place associatively, on the basis of his rich knowledge of Western history and theory of architecture and city.

3
Toronto, original plan of the BCE Place Galeria and Heritage Square, 1987–92.

4
Barcelona, view of the Bach de Roda Bridge (1985–87).

5
Valencia, site plan of the Science and Technology Museum (1991).

Bernhard Klein

5

Calatrava feels intuitively that what we term urban planning in its historical context has, for the past two hundred years, been anything but the urban architecture of Christopher Wren or Richard Newcourt, citing the example of the reconstruction of the City of London after the Great Fire of 1666. He also senses that these 'city-like structures', surviving merely as mummified forms of a *heavenly Jerusalem*, have just become traffic jams since the liberalism of the first half of the 19th century, 'ruled and orchestrated' from the furthest flung corners of the world – not, however, self-governed by their own citizens. The stations and station projects for Lucerne, Zürich-Stadelhofen, Berlin-Spandau and Lyon-Satolas represent the realisation that cities as a focus of political power have run their course, that they have degenerated into mere centres for political, economic and cultural units of administration within the state. Thus, no architectural practice can make sense if it bases itself on a higher urban culture in order to domesticate a lower rural culture. Cities, dissolved into housing estates, cannot support *Urban Architecture*, as Aldo Rossi[7] so momentously outlined in 1966. This Comédie Humaine, for example as described (for the 18th century in such a graphic way) by Richard Sennett[8], is no longer experienced as reality, and Calatrava refuses to offer its remnants like relics upon the altar of Western urban culture. The architects of the neo-rationalistic school play a considerable part in the ritual of these offerings.

This reversion has occurred because the architects of CIAM-Functionalism, which borders on the vulgar, have been forced into a corner by the 1960's 'pressure of the street'. Never before has there been a time when planning has been undertaken so extensively, and without public commission – a time when the architect has manoeuvered himself into the position of being his own boss: Echternach, Venice, Rome … the projects develop themselves first of all within the triangulation of Typology, Morphology and History, but in the end the complimentary discussion concerns itself only with the portrayal of associative freedoms within architecture. The city, however, was just as beyond rescue with this discussion of image as it was through Jane Jacobs'[9] rousing theses of 1963. The city had become anything other than a continuous process.

Alongside this as yet unresolved, and until now unmastered change in mentality comes, of all things, a new kind of explaining and simultaneously educating monumentality – a monumentality reminiscent of the restless mood of French architects in the decades before the French Revolution.

III

Gradually, in line with an urbanised post industrial society, urban landscapes achieve another character as a result of Calatrava's interventions, less in the intricacy of the façade, more in the overall view of urban reality. This urban revolution, which Calatrava appears to grasp from the periphery more clearly than others who stand at the cultural centre of the theatre of operation *City*, and which he transforms through his characteristic planning methods, stirs up the helplessness of urbanists from neo-rationalist to deconstructivist hue. The provisional culminating point of this confrontation, transferred from the urban–rural conflict into the discussion of periphery, is Calatrava's airport railway station in Satolas, near Lyon (6).

From the point of view of the competition jury, a monument was demanded for the establishment of a point of architectonic punctuation in the 'No-man's land' between city and countryside. It could be suggested that a kind of repair to the peripheral city form had been conceived, in the form of a linked chain of buildings similar to the customs line for Paris built by Claude-Nicolas Ledoux in the 1880's in response to Marc-Antoine Laugier's criticism of the village-like appearance of the Paris city limits. Calatrava's solution for the Lyon station hall is to be measured against these urban architectural programs, and not against neo-rationalistic typology. According to a kind of conditioned typology of buildings along a

6

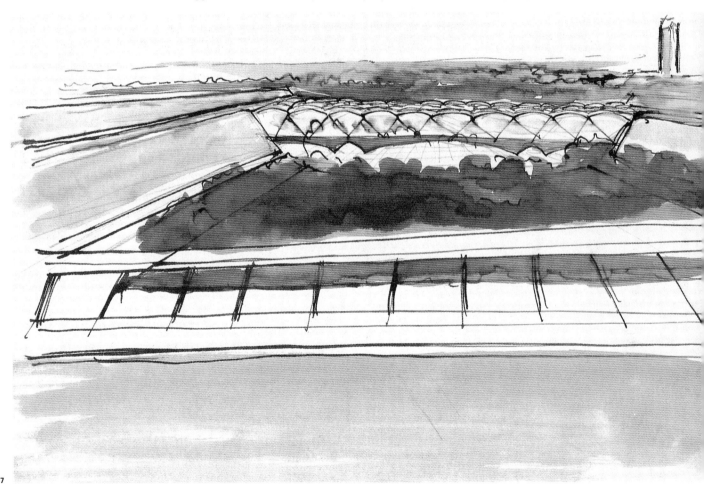

7

borderline, Ledoux was not allowed the selection of a *villae suburbanae* as a model for his Paris customs buildings. In this way, design according to typology is also in blatant contrast to Calatrava's efforts in formulating a revolutionary station serving as a place where one remains for the shortest time, and needing no pseudo-sacred dignity.

With Satolas, an until now unachieved *tour de force*, with the mastery of the amorphous appearance of the periphery, has been set in place. At the same time, Satolas advances towards the centre of the *settlement area* of Lyon, whilst the *city core* experiences a clear diminishing of role. The extension of the rail network to Marseille demands a diversion around Lyon centre and eventually makes the Paris–Marseille connection possible without a stop in Lyon; trains travel through the tunnel beneath the station hall. In Satolas, all ideas worked out in earlier projects have been convertible to a larger scale. At the same time, insights into the correct approach towards the phenomenon of the city move ever more into the observer's field of view. With the competition project for the Berlin-Spandau railway station, Calatrava adopts the theme of big city design, for many years multifariously discussed, which resists with the urban sophistication of open structures the history-obscuring effort to heal the wounds of war and reconstruction (7, 8). The thinking (apparently not 'big city' thinking according to the neo-rationalist interpretation), which, instead of complementing street alignment promotes the design of a bridge-like architecture under and through which 'open city spaces' such as parks

can expand, has its earliest roots at the district level with Zürich Stadelhofen, and will, as a consequence, be further developed in the big city perimeter of Berlin.

It is typical of Calatrava that, for example, in the framework of this competition he does not draw the kind of site plans which serve the neo-rationalists as proof of contextual design as fixed by the headlines 'Continuity' and 'Permanence'. It is much more through design work on the model that Calatrava eventually reaches a high degree of abstraction from traces of urban planning – a far more important result than his until now clearly recognisable formal allusions to architectonic references. What the eyes of architects released from the neo-rationalistic schools fail to see when searching for 'Permanence' in the site plan are just those phenomena which – totally and utterly apositivist – only allow themselves to be grasped through adaptive, inductive and, finally, deductive steps of analysis and design. Fundamental here are the mechanisms for dissolving the closed harmony of the city, which have been emerging since about 1750. This development is in spite of the almost aggressive efforts towards reconstruction of the older historical parts of cities in order to give them a 'heart'[10]. This found an expression in the ideas of open city space, for example. The application of the ideas of the open city area into the region, although not into the whole country, was the way in which these ideas manifested themselves in Calatrava's projects for Berlin-Spandau and Lyon-Satolas. It has had a significant effect on urban planning. Obviously, historical city cores can no longer be interpreted as crowns in

8

6
Lyon-Satolas, sketch, 1989.

7
Berlin-Spandau, watercolour, 1991.

8
Berlin-Spandau, watercolour, 1991.

Bernhard Klein

the landscape, as they are understood in a sweeping sense by politics, economics and culture[11], nor can this landscape be understood merely as a leisure area for activities radiating out from the city centre, certainly not if we are aware of the almost two-hundred-year-long transition from a closed into an open society which is now drawing to an end. Interestingly, in spite of all the progress within disciplines such as politics, sociology and economics which border on

10

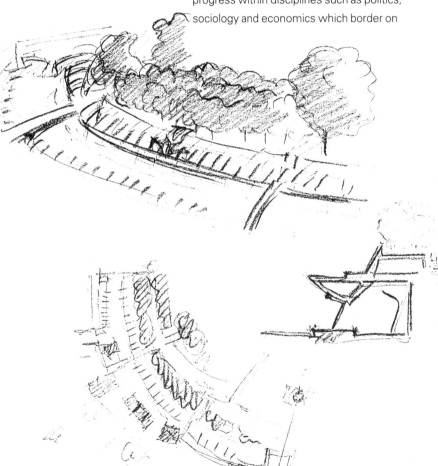

9

architecture and urban planning only the image of a new urbanity is perceived; the fundamental urban theories are not, however, formulated. Far removed from a somehow conditioned notion of Utopia, Calatrava's architectonic constructions have the quality of a new, though not yet discussed, solution to urban planning, namely, a *nebulous city*, consequently deriving from a dissolution of the closed, harmonising city form.

IV

But where do the roots of Calatrava's intuitive sureness lie when dealing with the city of the closing years of the 20th century?

His architectural and urbanistic education was at the Escuela Technica Superior de Arquitectura de Valencia (1969–73), the cultural alignment of which is mainly recognisable in his verbal and lucidly drawn allusions to Leonardo da Vinci and Michelangelo. The inherent ambivalence of statics and movement in their drawings, and also in the great halls of the 19th century – spaces for machines which devour space, constituting the fascination of the railway station – is taken up and corrected by Calatrava, in that the technical demonstration of the domination of statics is placed above their glorification. In Satolas, near Lyon, Calatrava builds the hall for the users of the station, and not for the machines; in Zürich Stadelhofen he dispenses completely with an interpretation of the traditional architectural station prototype (9). Stadelhofen stands at the beginning of his 'anti-utopia': an anti-place, creating a new kind of urbanism; an anti-type creating another

12

notion of architecture and city. Throughout a wide spectrum of the population it is clear, in connection with the considerable planning difficulties surrounding the multi-functional main Zürich station, that Calatrava's Stadelhofen does not correspond to the 19th century station prototype. Apart from the urban inner space of a shopping passage on the lower floor, which was not anticipated in the competition project, Calatrava restricts himself to the architectonic, well conceived circulatory systems, which, in spite of considerable interference, allow the site to appear remarkably undeveloped and, moreover, enhance the previously existing and conservationalist protected anti-place. In order to elucidate on the transdisciplinary in Calatrava's work using a known example, Brunelleschi's solution for the Florentine cathedral dome has been referred to[12]. But Brunelleschi was that same architect who, as the father figure of the monumental buildings of socialistic realism, became a scapegoat. Monumentalism as an expression of social change? Florence became a different city as a result of Brunelleschi's interference, a change of meaning which could well be described as a new

11

9
Zürich, sketches of Stadelhofen Station.

10
East London River Crossing, 1990.

11
Salginatobel Bridge, Maillart, Grisons, 1928. Photograph: David P. Billington.

12
Scotland. Railway viaduct by Leaderfoot.

foundation. Monumentalism in the 19th century is to be seen against the background of the nationalistic idea. In order to be able to appear carefree alongside other forms of architecture, in the sense of the politics of the empty space, monuments were created – zero points of urban reality – which in no way differ from Mitterand's planning of the eighties and nineties.

Not only with Calatrava's station projects does a new monumentality extend through urban space, giving voice to a change in social reality. Calatrava suggests another kind of 'Elegance and Dignity' to the hierarchal reality promoted by HRH The Prince of Wales on 1.12.1987 as being 'the real heart of the capital' in the planning concept for the new development of Paternoster Square, opposite St. Paul's Cathedral – namely, an integral reality, as Calatrava also suggests for the East London River Crossing (10). As opposed to aristocratic dilettantism, intent on reconstructing a city feudalism, Calatrava recognises the socio-economic forces which mark our settlement areas and searches for an adequate monumentalisation[14]. After London finally lost its traditional silhouette after 1960, and after St. Paul's had been submerged in a tide of high-rise buildings[15], Calatrava introduced a new monumental dimension with his project for the East London River Crossing. Its distinctiveness realigns the city's form, fully comparable with the significance of Maillart's Salginatobel bridge[16] of 1928 to the legibility of the landscape (11). In contrast, it is clear that the endless addition of here a brick-arched bridge, or there a railway viaduct by Leaderfoot, can no longer provide scale[17](12).

V

Calatrava creates no theory of architecture; he designs and builds. The analysis of his buildings does, however, show an obvious stringency: from the start, an idea is consequently furthered, an idea which is not borrowed from the Durand-ish rationalism of the post-war era, nor from the pictorial world of the (post-)moderns. His archetypes are taken from a world which does not form hierarchies of reactionary alignment. What Calatrava characterises with dynamic equilibrium means solely that the element of form, still so monumental in appearance, cannot shape a coherent system without its thin tensioned cable. For architects who indeed have not had the classical Beaux-Arts education, but in the end always revert to quoting classical architectural theory, the decision to make the motif for a bridge-head sculpture or a penthouse library repeat in an airport or city railway station lies beyond the realms of their imagination!

Adequate principles of construction and mechanics are in particular at the centre of interest and point clearly to the time when no difference could be drawn between architect and engineer. Firstly, it doesn't therefore involve a decision – architect, or engineer? Calatrava doesn't let himself get pinned down. Secondly, it has nothing to do with the organic. The skeleton of an animal is not a treasury of form, it serves only to clarify the connectedness of its parts, finally assisting in the stability of movement. The skeleton is similarly recognisable in the gothic constructions where the envelope encloses completely, while the skin allows the bones to shine through. It has nothing to do with the form of the bones. What counts is the subjectivity of feeling about mechanical principles which gives security in the presence of an enacted dynamic equilibrium. According to Ludwig Wittgenstein, every statement is an image and this image is not to be separated from form. 'Architecture is in a position to convert thoughts into clearly depicted form, whilst philosophy does not possess this possibility to the same degree…architecture… is a means of creating clear and final forms, to which nothing can be added or removed without disturbing, or even destroying the result.'[18] In '*Eupolinos or the architect*', Paul Valéry attempted in 1921 to elevate architecture to the level of philosophy.

With the thirties, and with Valéry's Eupolinos, Calatrava combines a trust in the possibility of overcoming the urban grievance, and of educating mankind. The psychogogic significance of architecture appears, as in the thirties, to reawaken in Calatrava's singing monuments, which do not restrict themselves to the individual emotions they inspire but rather communicate a collective message. And this collective message means to say that the modern concept of *Urbanismus der Solitare* wants to achieve the recovery of the whole through the quality of the individual object, and not through a resuscitation of the integrating, historical figure.

Translated from the German by Dennis Gartrell.

Footnotes

1 *Valéry*, Paul, *Eupolinos oder der Architekt*, translated by Rainer Maria Rilke, Frankfurt am Main 1973, p. 80 (Original French edition: Eupolinos ou l'Architecte, Paris, 1923).
2 'Trifles' refers to carefully sanitised historic buildings, cosseted by the conservationists, which were originally generously conceived, and not based on colloquial models.
3 The old Jewish civic hall at 79–80 Fasanenstrasse, Berlin-Charlottenburg, should also be born in mind. The portal of the original synagogue was included in the rebuilding in remembrance of its destruction and as a symbol of interrupted continuity. (See Both, Rolf (Publisher), *Synagogues in Berlin: The history of a destroyed architecture*. Part 2 (Catalogue of the exhibition held at The Berlin Museum from 26 January to 20 March 1983), Berlin 1983, page 114, Fig 106a). War memorials have also been created with a similar concept, for example the Berlin Kaiser-Wilhelm-Gedächtniskirche by Egon Eiermann.
4 *Blaser*, Werner, *Santiago Calatrava: Engineering Architect*, Birkhäuser, 2nd edition, Basel Boston Berlin 1990, page 30.
5 'Defortification' as a result of developments in artillery is an inadequate explanation of the changes in boundary between a city and its environs. Is the erosion of the border an effect of physiocratic economic and social theory of the second half of the 18th century? See *Klein*, Bernhard. *Die physiokratische Verlandschaftung der Stadt um 1800: Städtebau und Stadtauflösung in der Realität von Freiburg im Breisgau sowie in der Utopie des französischen Revolutionsarchitekten Ledoux* (1990).
6 The term *Nebulous City*, as an aid, can be traced back to Jean Gottmann's enquiries into the New York-Washington conurbation. In the sixties he characterised this as 'Nebulous', (my thanks to Prof. André Corboz, ETH-Zürich, for pointing this out). Almost no scientific interest has until now been shown in this phenomenon of the *nebulous city*, which its author has attempted to expound in a series of unpublished lectures and opinions concerning the critique of buildings and projects from their city planning perspective. This is probably all the more so, because prevalent hierarchical thinking hinders an integral way of thought coherent to the concept of nebulous cities, making them impossible, even.
7 *Rossi*, Aldo, *Die Architektur der Stadt: Skizze zu einer grundlegenden Theorie des Urbanen*, Düsseldorf 1973 (Original title: L'Architettura della Città, Padova 1966).
8 *Sennett*, Richard, *The Fall of Public Man*, New York 1974.
9 *Jacobs*, Jane, *The Death and Life of Great American Cities*, New York 1961.
10 The conception of 'Heart of the City', formulated in 1952 as an abandonment of the ideas about cities as represented by the Congrès Internationaux d'Architecture Moderne (CIAM), was cleverly reconstrued in their interest in the middle of the seventies through preservation. See *Tyrwhitt*, J., *Sert*, J.L. and *Rogers*, E., *The Heart of the City*, London 1952.
11 A role not to be underestimated, until now appearing to have found no expression in research, and here adopted by Karl Gruber. See *Gruber*, Karl, *Die Gestalt der deutschen Stadt: Ihr Wandel aus der geistigen Ordnung der Zeiten*, Munich 1952.
12 See *Meckseper*, Cord, *Laudatio auf Dr. Santiago Calatrava-Valls*, in: Stiftung F.V.S. Zu Hamburg (Publisher), Fritz-Schumacher-Stiftung 1988, pages 17–19.
13 See *Corboz*. André, *Über Wiedergrundungen oder Stadtkernforschung einmal anders*, in: Corboz, André (Pub.): *Die Stadt mit Eigenschaften, Eine Hommage an Paul Hofer*, Zürich 1991 (published in autumn 1991).
14 See *HRH The Prince of Wales, A Vision of Britain*, London 1989, p. 69–74.
15 See *HRH The Prince of Wales: A Vision of Britain*, London 1989.
16 See *Billington, Robert Maillart's Bridges*, Princeton, 1979. pp. 77–90.
17 See *HRH The Prince of Wales, A Vision of Britain*, London 1989, p. 19.
18 *Borsi*, Franco, *Die Monumentale Ordnung. Architektur in Europa 1929–1939*, Stuttgart 1987.

Bernhard Klein

Anthony Tischhauser

Santiago Calatrava: An Eye for the Curve

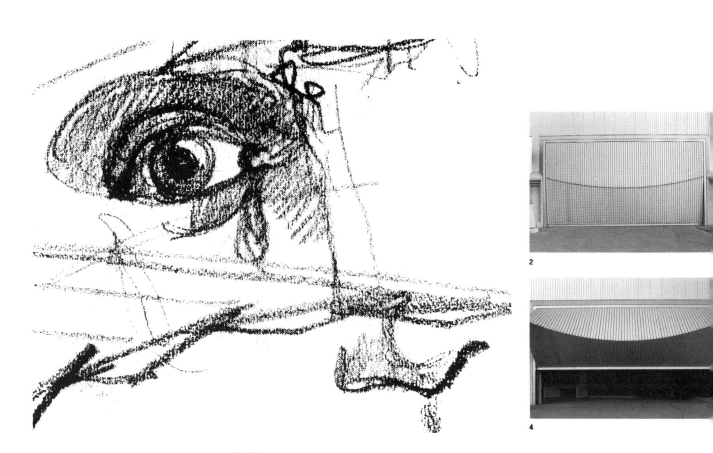

2

4

There is no such thing as a straight line in nature, so the curve comes quite naturally to Santiago Calatrava. He will give any function a shape. He doesn't create a curve to catch the eye. He sees the curve in the way he sees light in the eye. His continuous sketching is a document of his fascination for the unfolding of the lid over the eyeball – an elliptical curve held in tension. The eye of the seer and seen – this organ of light is a continuous source of inspiration and one of his most expressed images.

Santiago Calatrava is a truly architectural architect. He breathes life into design. He does not conform to the intellectually acquired process stifling modern architecture. Through his eye for the curve he helps us make new discoveries. The striving after beauty arises out of a polarity. Beauty exists on the borderline of the tangible and ethereal, on the borderline between the temporal and causal world. It is an echo of the one source that we cannot otherwise grasp. Calatrava's work is created in the knowledge that there is an almost unbearable tension between our understanding of the world and our expression of it. His buildings reflect this tension.

Calatrava's curves thus express movement through the interplay of light and darkness. They express the rhythmic flow of moving changing forms in both continuity and the dynamics of contrast. Aspects of form recognised in the abundance of nature are the source of his continuing idea and lead us beyond the sense-bound experience of space and light.
In his quest for beauty, Calatrava will design a

symmetrical bow in spanned tension over the River Seine in Paris. Pont Gentil, approached from land, is asymmetric – the arch swooping, tilted in the direction of the water's flow, in order to counterbalance the vehicle and pedestrian deck (1). To complicate this balancing act, metro tracks are cantilevered off the deck, beneath the arch. The principle of shifting the arch to the edge of the bridge and rotating it to lean is a strong image that cocks a snook at conventional notions on equilibrium. This was realised in the extraordinarily light structure of the 'La Devesa' Bridge in Ripoll, Spain. The shaft of the Alamillo Bridge, with its arm reaching over the Meandro San Jerónimo river bank, has also been tilted to its point of equilibrium, its sheer size commenting on the relationship of tension and mass. To Calatrava, a bridge is not only an object of beauty, it is also a feat of engineering. A bridge is a statement about the nature of a bridge. It is an essay, an individual gesture, and should not be subservient to the barren modern idea of standardised production.

At Ernsting's, the secret of the doors, once again lies in the curve of the eye (2, 3, 4, 5). When closed, the flow of the hinge line curve can be detected across each. Closer inspection reveals that each joint of the aluminium slats is staggered. These delivery bay doors fold into eyelashes, becoming canopies. Entrance to the Montjuïc Tower is through an eye-opening, where the door likewise folds, but in reverse. Calatrava's structures allude to transformation through movement. The key to any even merely implied movement between static elements is the joint. This centre of movement, this point of rotation, is

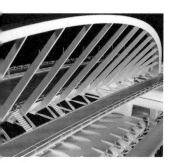

1

3

5

Anthony Tischhauser | 25

6

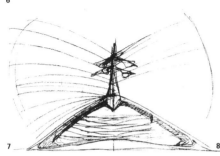

7

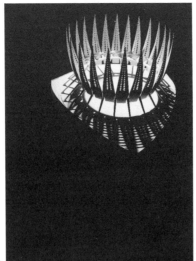

8

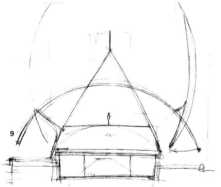

9

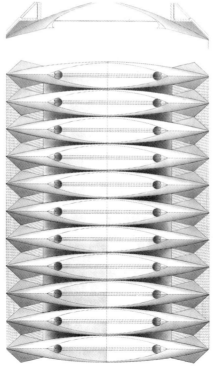

10

a feature treated with aesthetic care.

For the ceiling in Muri Cloister, Switzerland, the eyelid gives way to a wave-like movement of timber slats suspended from the existing roof structure – and frozen. These captive curves are then freed and set in motion in Basle. For the Cement Industry's Pavilion at the 'Swissbau' building fair, Calatrava cast huge bones in concrete. Their ultra-fine surface is uncanny, almost like velvet. The 1.2-ton elements, set in slow motion, imitate each other in a rhythmical curve, like the beat of a wing.

For the same industry's pavilion on the Lake of Lucerne, a floating flower structure is proposed where pierced petals arranged in a circle can be moved individually (6, 7, 8). The blades lift up to beyond the vertical in a rhythmic centrifugal pattern. The variations are innumerable, a circular eye and yet a swan in flight with wings outstretched. These long palm-like slithers were eventually realised for the Kuwaiti Pavilion at Expo '92 in Seville (9).

Calatrava is a place maker. He will see the opportunity in any task for creating a place. The flying 'piazza' protruding elliptically from the lean-to arches on the Bach de Roda Bridge permits the eye a view of the parks on either side of the railway. In Paris, the Solferino Bridge becomes a viewing platform over the River Seine between the Louvre and the Musée d'Orsay. Stairs are always a place between borders. A two-tier stair leads to the balcony for viewing the square from the Falkensteg Bridge at Stadelhofen.

Like a cyclist curving rhythmically on a road along

Anthony Tischhauser | **26**

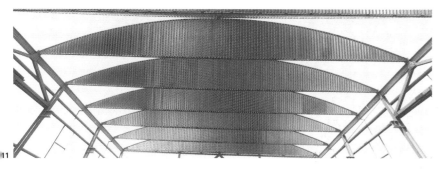

an imaginary axis, Calatrava takes a swoop, thus creating an accelerated flowing curve between the point of support and its thrust. The Oglasteg loosely spans the 'vaulting pole' at Stadelhofen. The roof for the multi-purpose hall in Suhr, Switzerland, is another example, with tensioned cables piercing eyes set in curved ceiling panels jointed at the point of maximum stress (10). The first use of the eye-curve evolved with the Jakem Factory, where the leaf-like curve apparently follows the lines of force of the triangular trusses (11). This is Calatrava at work.

12

He has an eye for the curve that is unique. It cannot be imitated, it is the way he instinctively sees. Calatrava is remarkable in his ability to make a curve work as a sketch and at the same time be intrinsically beautiful, whilst remaining convincing even when translated into another medium and passing through the hands of several others. How does Calatrava manage to maintain a sense of liveliness during this transformation into three dimensions? It is the quality of inspiration that fires the mind and entices. This explains Calatrava's respect for craftsmanship. He both demands it and practices it. The aesthetic feeling is constantly nurtured in a sketch, drawing, model or detail. In the same way as a musician, Calatrava practices every day to 'keep in tune'. He listens carefully, comparing atmospheric rhythms and harmonies. The bridge of the violin has inspired several of his cable-stayed bridges. In tuning the image, the pylon might be bent under the force of the strings and then also bent as homage to the eye.
He will see the curve of a bridge and design it to be completed by the water reflection. The triple

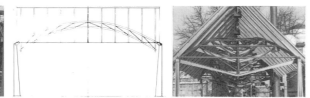

13

14

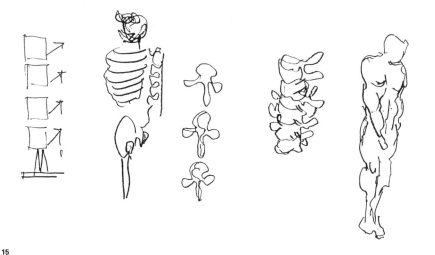

rhythmic hop of the Wettstein Bridge over existing abutments at the foot of the cathedral in Basle is marked by the concaves of pinched arches (12). This idea was first seen in a traditional bus stop shelter in St. Gallen. Like a thrust of vertebrae the inclined arches are hidden under the glass skin roof (13). Wohlen High School is entered through the bridge of an eye with glass lashes upturned (14, 16). Calatrava has said that Stadelhofen is merely a collection of bridges. In Spandau the urban park is bridged over to create the railway station.

Calatrava's buildings don't impose on a landscape or a cityscape. They are respectful of the fact that the world was there first. They don't demand space, they enhance it. They don't fill space, they give it meaning – a new dimension to the landscape, opening new horizons. The seeming transparent lightness of a heavy structure creates energy and Calatrava invites us to cross a barrier. Calatrava uses self-finished and self-coloured materials. They are not stock materials, but compounded from stock with the cut and weld of a computer or the blend of particular sands. The texture of concrete, steel and glass is expressed through the weight of the materials brought to bear, the heaviness expressed not necessarily being real. The 'violence of the joint' is fundamental with the concrete curve of the Stadelhofen promenade holding the steel supports in place. Steel is often made to seem lighter and heavy granite stones can appear even heavier when contrasted with the slender chromium cable, balanced on thin cones. This can be clearly observed in the 'Torso' and 'Toros'

16

15
Toros, 1985, sculpture. Early sketches.

16
Wohlen High School hall roof structure,
Wohlen, 1984–89.

17
9 October Bridge, Valencia,
1985–87.

18
Concert Hall, Santa Cruz, Tenerife,
1991. Detail of early sketch.

series of sculptures (15). The look of the material is skin-deep, when smooth-bonded concrete supports the exposed rough fibres of wooden parabolic curves of the Wohlen school hall (16). A sublime atmosphere is contrasted by rough hewn floor slate. Polished glass stairs leading up to Tabourettli Theatre appear with an added layer of white exquisite marble as a continuous curved floor to the Kuwaiti Pavilion.

Calatrava's deep respect for the force of life is expressed in terms of equilibrium which he best observes in the human body. Some of these images appear directly transmitted in pictorial terms, others attempt to geometricise human poses in his quest to understand a wider dimension of the forces at work. Figures in tension serve as a cue. A hand supporting a private library roof is then used at Stadelhofen to hold the promenade, three fingers grasp the glass canopy. The gesture of the hand also holds the eye of the Onidia Table Lamp. With a hawk's eye for proportion a jump in scale merely requires an adjustment of feeling and weight. His structures give the impression of being built of sections strung together, having first unfolded in the eye of the mind. They are not unfolding systems, but movement drawn out into form. A commission will be tested against previously conceived phenomena. The impression is not necessarily the development of an idea to build, but the building of an idea while unfolding creative power. Calatrava's qualitative grasp of form in many cases reaches out to the experience of geometrical metamorphosis. One curve blends into another without losing its identity. We are helped to

understand a creative process taking place in time, penetrating behind the fixed form and arising out of a juxtaposition. The form is apprehended long before it materialises and is fixed as a shape in space in the quantitive field of measurement. Drawing on the rhetoric of the eye the fractal sculpture 'The Bird' is seen, transposed into a beacon for the 'Ninth of October' Bridge (17). From the view of a bird's eye it perches over the track at Lyon in full plume. The bird of the concert hall in Santa Cruz unfolds liberating empathy, while tantalizing gravity (18).

Calatrava is both scientist and artist. With the wink of an eye and through experiment he lets his creatures evolve. With astonishing speed and precision a curve is given scale and spatial character. Rules and conventions make little impact on him and he demonstrates an anarchic trait towards discussion on architecture. He will speak in images and make his point through a fable or anecdote. His unorthodox use of the classic repertoire of humanist principles is expressed through the canons and devices of modern art. He could be called a Classical architect, although he is a man of his times, striving to transcend them. Buildings are like living beings to Calatrava and are treated as entities – they have a top and a bottom, an upper side and an under side, a beginning and an end. His buildings are legible and appear simple, clear and self-contained – concerned with the whole. Calatrava's humanistically based imagination leads him back to basic principles of harmony and balance. With a keen eye he starts each object anew, expressing it in the rhythmic flow of moving, changing curves.

Anthony Tischhauser

Santiago Calatrava:

Lyon Airport Railway Station

Buildings, Bridges and Projects

The scheme for Zürich's new Stadelhofen Railway Station arose as a result of a competition held in 1983 with Arnold Amsler and Walter Ruegger.

The station is located at the foot of a park-like hill which marks the edge of the old city's fortifications, next to the square in front of the Opera House. The project is distinguished not only by its structural ingenuity, but also by its urban contribution, in that it attempts to instil a familiar location with a modern and highly distinctive sense of place. The Stadelhofen project is a typical 'design by section'. The three-level cross section remains almost identical throughout its curving 270 m length, which follows the line of the hill. The apparently complex structure can be broken down into a simple vocabulary of individual components, combined and repeated to unite the disparate elements of the station as a homogenous, urban whole. Three platforms run the length of the railway tracks. On one side a high protective wall is set back

Previous page – the supple, curvaceous canopy evokes appropriate transport metaphors such as movement, strength and speed.

1
The station follows the line of existing tracks. A series of bridges penetrates the upper level walkway.

2
Site plan.

3
Model showing the relationship between the hillside residential area and the new station. The project aims to impart a new sense of identity to a familiar civic location.

4
Detail of canopy model, which has a strange, organic quality, like the skeletal remains of some prehistoric behemoth.

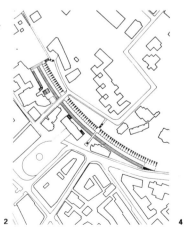

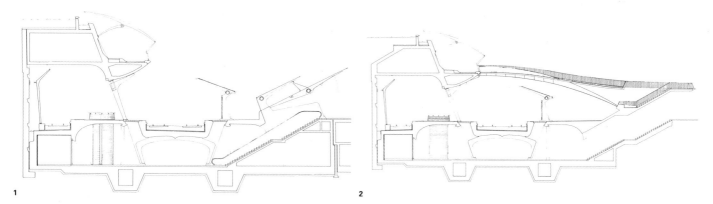

1

2

3

1
Cross section through staircase.

2
Cross section through platforms and bridge link at upper level.

3
Detail of bridge/walkway interface.

4
The scheme is conceived as a multi-layered section that remains virtually unchanged along its entire 270 m length.

5
The upper level walkway affords good views over the city.

6
Elevation of the upper level walkway.

7
Two platforms are linked at lower level by a crepuscular basement.

4

Stadelhofen Station, Zürich |

from the platform, with a generous loggia at the upper level; on the other a freestanding canopy with an elegantly cantilevered glass roof. The three platforms are linked at the lower level by a basement underpass, which also contains a parade of shops, and at the upper level by four separate bridge connections. The upper promenade is conceived as an enfilade of light arched steel pergolas with wires strung between them, which will eventually sustain a translucent covering of greenery. Calatrava's notion of structure as a form of petrified movement is evident throughout Stadelhofen, from the tripartite Y-shaped column heads carrying the steel and glass canopy over the original platform, to the vertiginously inclined pergolas on the upper promenade. There is also a characteristic anatomical quality to the structural element, particularly in the basement arcade, suggestive of an enormous concrete rib cage and the freestanding canopy like a skeletal dinosaur's tail. The prevalence of such biomorphism inevitably encourages comparisons with fellow Catalan Antonio Gaudí, but Calatrava's precise structural expressionism has, as critic Kenneth Frampton suggests, its origins in the perpetual Germanic fascination with technology. At Stadelhofen this technology has a crucial human and civic dimension, elevating a busy branch station to a form of dynamic urban sculpture.

5

6

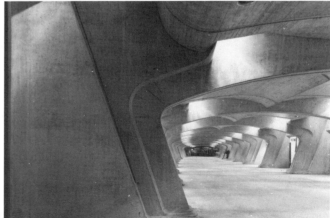

7

Stadelhofen Station, Zürich | 35

This page - detail of the massive steel arch that spans 189m.

1
Location plan. The bridge connects the old town of Merida with Poligono.

2
Elevation and site plan.

3
Detail of model.

4
The new structure under construction, viewed from the town's original Roman bridge, now given over to pedestrian use.

Lusitania Bridge, Merida 1988 - 91

The Lusitania Bridge connects the old town of Merida with the newly developed area of Poligono on the northern side of the river Guadiana in western Spain. The river bed is some 500 m wide and the bridge's dimensions are correspondingly generous, yet the structure has a simple, elegant fluidity. The new crossing is located 600 m downstream from the town's original Roman bridge, now allocated solely for pedestrian use. The implicit challenge posed by the 2000-year-old structure is met by a rhythmic repetition of loadbearing elements in the three zones of the new bridge. The most expressive structural element is a huge steel arch 34 m high, that spans 189 m. Pedestrian and car routes are separated, with the central pedestrian level raised 1.5 m above the dual carriageway on either side. Post-stressed concrete wings are cantilevered from the 4.45 m deep concrete box girder spine to form the bridge deck and the upper surface of the box girder serves as the pedestrian walkway.

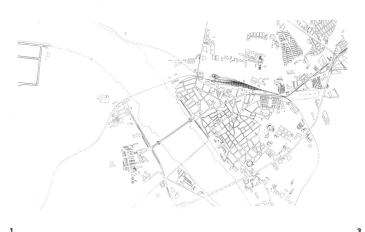

1

3

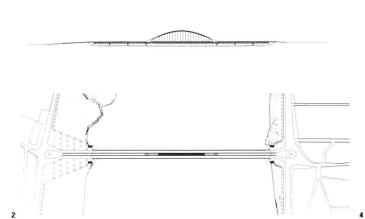

2

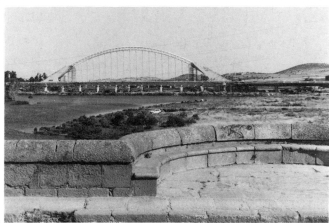

4

1

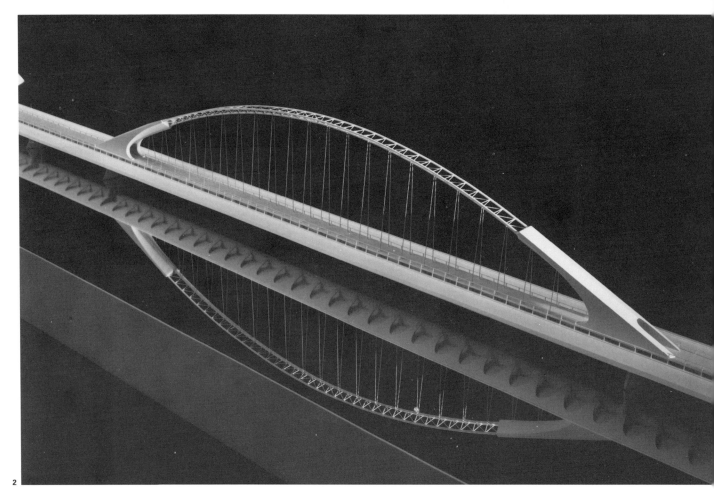

2

Lusitania Bridge, Merida | 38

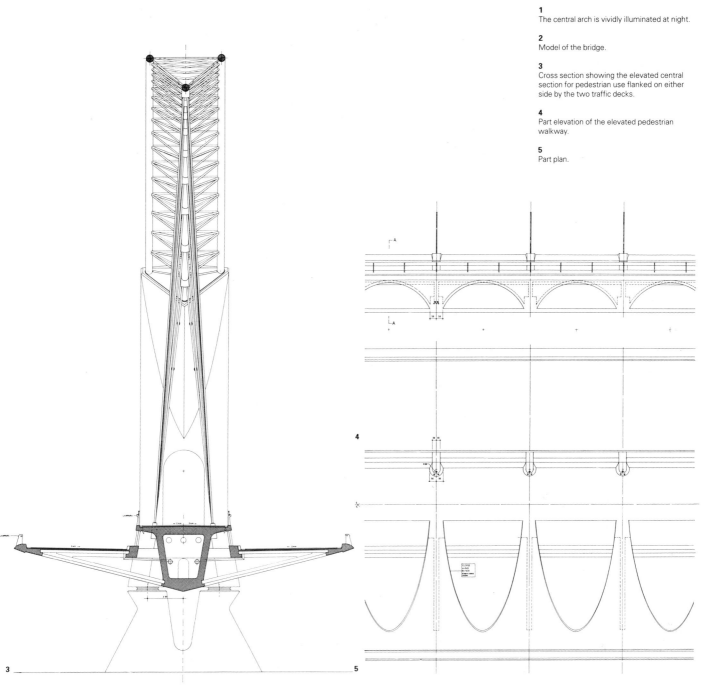

1
The central arch is vividly illuminated at night.

2
Model of the bridge.

3
Cross section showing the elevated central section for pedestrian use flanked on either side by the two traffic decks.

4
Part elevation of the elevated pedestrian walkway.

5
Part plan.

3

4

5

Lusitania Bridge, Merida | 39

This page – the 142 m high inclined pylon gives the bridge a bold, sculptural dynamism. The weight of the steel clad and filled concrete pylon is sufficient to counterbalance the bridge deck.

1
Model of the original proposal for two symmetrical bridges and viaduct forming a monumental gateway at the north end of the Isla de la Cartuja.

2, 3
Details of the model.

The staging of Expo '92 in Seville prompted the civic authorities to undertake an ambitious series of improvements to the city's infrastructure. These included regional road connections, a ring road for Seville and eight new bridges over the river Guadalquivir. One of the new roads passes out of Seville to the north, across the Meandro San Jerónimo to the Isla de La Cartuja, skirting the Expo site and thereafter over the river Guadalquivir to the town of Camas in the west. The unusual situation of crossing the same river twice and the proximity to the Expo site called for a radical intervention. Two symmetrical bridges were proposed, each shaped like a giant harp and supported by a massive inclined pylon. Although 1.5 km apart, these would be angled towards one another to create a monumental gateway at the north end of the island. Ultimately, only one of the proposed bridges was built. The remarkable Alamillo Bridge spans 200 m across the Meandro San Jerónimo, supported by thirteen pairs of cable stays from a 142 m high pylon inclined at an angle of 58°. The bridge deck consists of a hexagonal steel box beam, to which the cables are attached. The steel wings that support the two carriageways are cantilevered off the beam and the top of the spine forms the elevated pedestrian walkway between the traffic lanes.

1

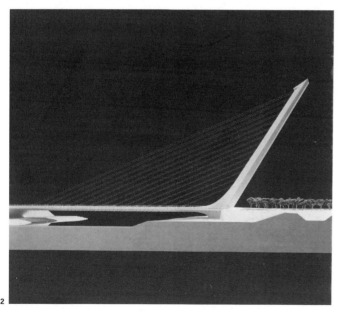

2

3

Alamillo Bridge, Seville | 41

1

2

Alamillo Bridge, Seville | 42

1
Crossing the elevated pedestrian walkway
at night is perhaps the most evocative way
to experience the bridge.

2
Project elevation (17 sets of cables).

3
Project cross section.

4
Detail of the steel cable stays. There are
thirteen pairs in all, giving the structure the
appearance of a giant harp.

5
Detail of one of the two traffic decks,
cantilevered off the central spine.

4

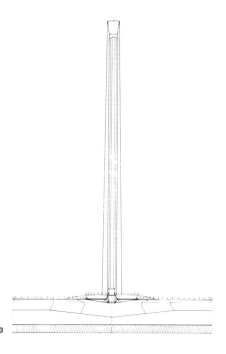

3

5

Alamillo Bridge, Seville | 43

This page – the dramatically inclined steel arch towers over the pedestrian deck.

1
Cross section showing the relationship between the arch and the cantilevered deck.

2
Elevation.

3
Plan.

4
The bridge in context. The total span is 65m.

5
Model of the scheme.

This pedestrian bridge spans the Rio Ter in the small Spanish town of Ripoll, just north of Barcelona. The 65 m long structure connects the railway station with the new development of La Devesa. The distinctive bow bridge comprises a tilted steel arch which supports a timber deck. However, this simple description belies the structural complexity involved. In an expressive asymmetrical arrangement of weight and counterweight, the single arch is placed on one side of the bridge deck and exaggeratedly tilted so as to seemingly counterbalance it. In effect, the deck is cantilevered off the arch, which is pivoted from underneath the bridge and slanted upwards at a dramatic level.

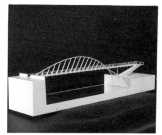

5

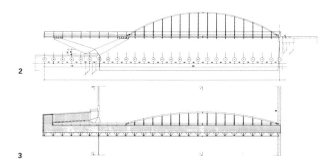

2

3

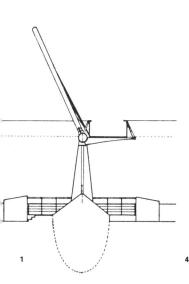

1

4

La Devesa Bridge, Ripoll | 45

1
Detail of the underside of the bridge showing how the deck structure is cantilevered off the main arch.

2
The arrangement of structural elements is expressively asymmetrical.

3
The exaggerated tilt of the arch appears to counterbalance the pedestrian deck.

3

La Devesa Bridge, Ripoll | 46

Constructed as part of Barcelona's preparations to stage the 1992 Olympic Games, Calatrava's unusually controversial telecommunications tower presides over the main group of sports facilities on the slopes of Montjuïc, providing the city with a monumental, if not entirely popular, new landmark. The tower lies next to the vast indoor sports arena designed by Arata Isozaki. A gently inclined concrete shaft rises up from a circular base, forks into two and is crowned by a semi-circular element housing the communications hardware. The entire structure is topped off with a vertical device that resembles a giant javelin suspended upright in mid air. Unfortunately, certain unenlightened modifications were made to the original design, notably the shortening of the main shaft. No compensatory adjustment was made to the crowning element, which must account, to some extent, for the tower's unsatisfactory proportions. In this respect, comparisons with the original scheme in model form are instructive.

This page – the new tower hovers surreally above the surrounding landscape on the hillside of Montjuic.

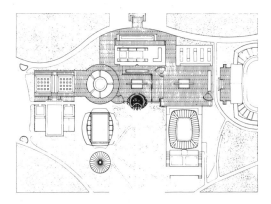

1

3

1
Site plan.

2
Plan of the base.

3
The tower in context, beside Arata Isozaki's
new indoor sports arena.

4
Model of the original scheme showing the
intended proportions of the various elements.
However, this bears little relationship to the
final built version. The length of the shaft
was subsequently shortened, with no
compensatory adjustment made to the size
of the crowning element.

2

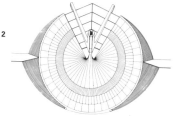

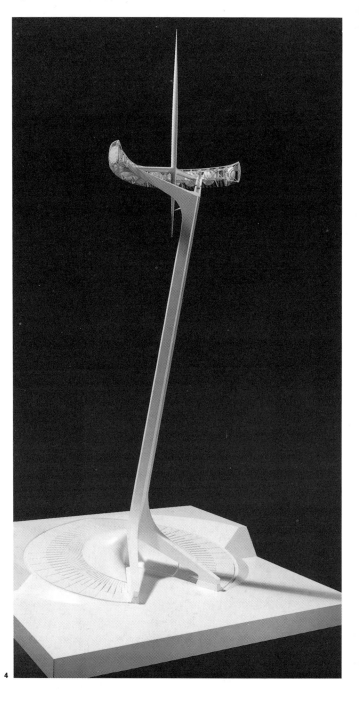

4

Montjuïc Communications Tower | **48**

This page - detail of the model, showing the intricate structure of the station hall.

One consequence of the preparations to host the 1992 Winter Olympics in Albertville was that the French high-speed train network (TGV), which will eventually run between Paris and Marseille, be extended to connect with Lyon airport. The station is currently under construction and in some ways marks a turning point in Calatrava's career, as the scheme is larger and possibly more complex than any realised project to date. Despite its daunting size. Lyon is essentially a monumental magnification of earlier roof and pavilion forms. The six tracks are enclosed by a 500 m long shallow-vaulted structure, criss-crossed with a lattice arrangement of concrete ribs. The platform vault is in turn surmounted at its midpoint by a station hall, reminiscent of a huge bird of prey with its wings outstretched. This analogy also recalls Eero Saarinen's iconographic TWA Terminal at Kennedy airport, although at Lyon Calatrava uses steel clad in aluminium as opposed to Saarinen's biomorphic concrete.

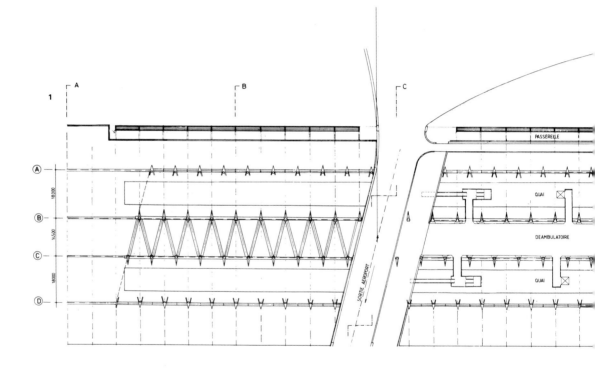

1
Plan.

2
West elevation. The shallow vault extends 500 m along the platforms. The station hall straddles the vault at its midpoint.

3
Detail of the model, showing how the station hall surmounts the low-slung lattice vault over the platforms.

2

Lyon Airport Railway Station

3

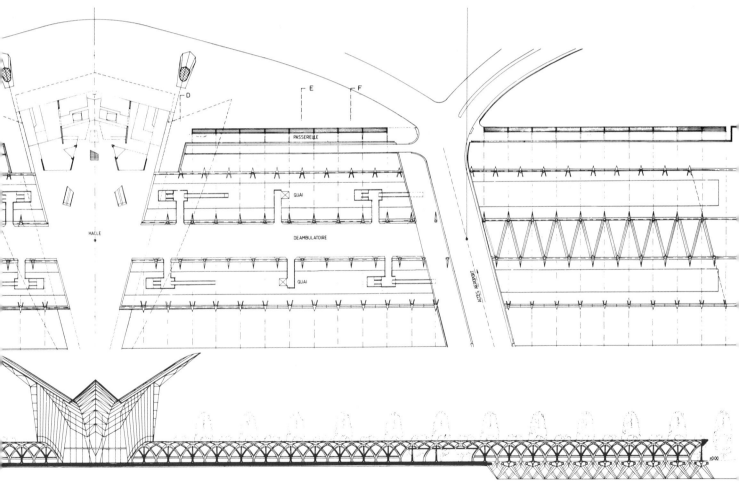

Lyon Airport Railway Station | 51

1

2

3

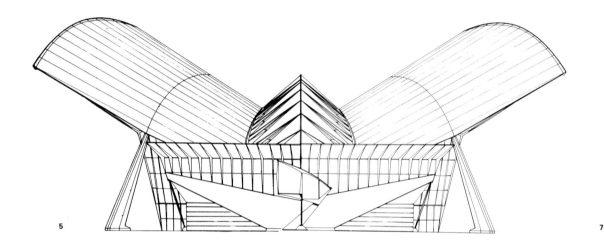

5

7

6

Lyon Airport Railway Station | 52

1–4
Site photographs showing the station under construction. It is expected to be completed next year.

5
Station hall, east elevation.

6
Station hall, west elevation.

7
Station hall, north elevation. From this angle, the taut curve of the structure seems clearly inspired by Calatrava's sculptural imagination.

8
Model showing detail of the station hall roof structure.

9
Model of part of the elevated walkway that links the TGV station with the main airport building.

Lyon Airport Railway Station | 53

1
West elevation of the main terminal building.

2
Cross section through the main terminal
building showing the conventional post and
beam structure which is used to give stability
to the dramatic curving roof.

3
Massing model (first phase).

4
Detailed model showing the airside elevation
and how the lateral wings relate to the main
terminal building (second phase).

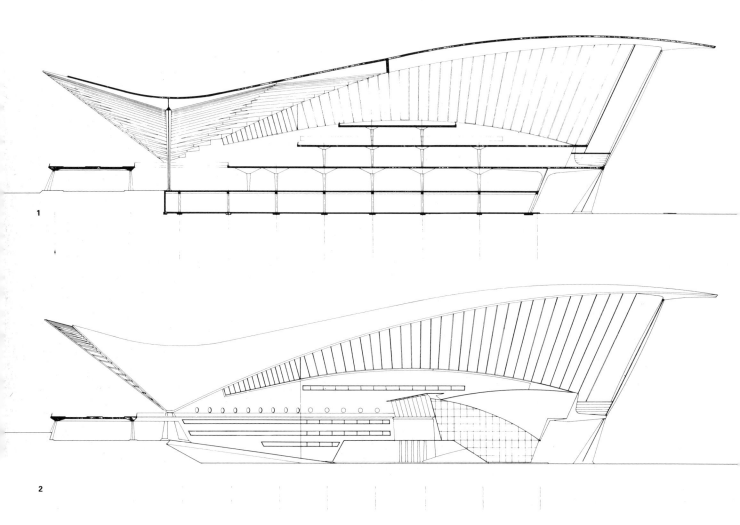

1

2

3

The new airport building in the northern Spanish port of Bilbao is another elegantly conceived metaphor for the dynamics of flight. The main terminal is arranged on four levels, with waiting areas for arrivals and departures located in two lateral wings. These are designed to allow for future expansion by progressively increasing the number of 'fingers' to serve the growing number of passengers. The structure of the main terminal building is a conventional concrete post and beam system, to give the necessary stability to the dramatic free-form roof. The steel-framed roof is based on an approximately triangular plan, supported by the inclined wall structure. For the two lateral wings, the double-cylindrical roof is formed by a series of steel ribs supported on longitudinal steel sections. Because of the transversal shape, the front part of the roof is variable and the back constant. The inclined façade is framed by a series of steel members supported by two concrete bearing arcs that transmit the structural forces to the ground.

Sondica Airport, Bilbao 1990 -

4

Sondica Airport | 55

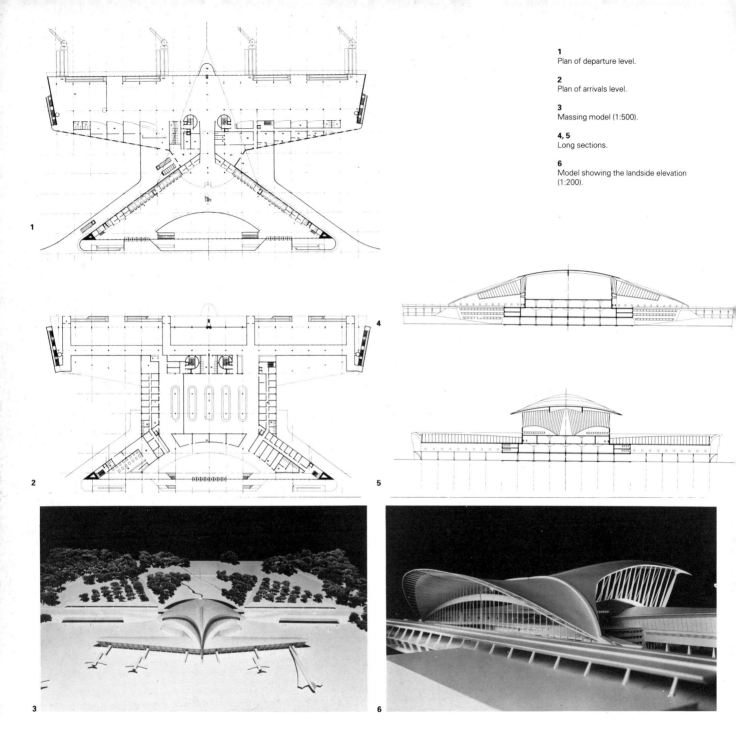

1
Plan of departure level.

2
Plan of arrivals level.

3
Massing model (1:500).

4, 5
Long sections.

6
Model showing the landside elevation
(1:200).

Sondica Airport | 56

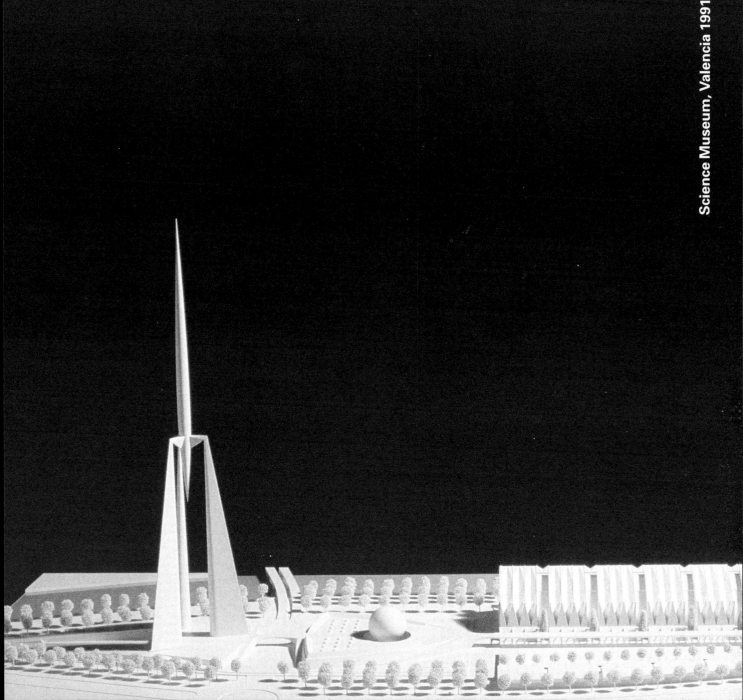

The tower in this scheme was the winning entry in a competition to design a huge science museum complex in Valencia. The science museum and planetarium were direct commissions. The elongated, eye-shaped site lies on the edge of the dried up River Turia, to the east of the old city centre. The various elements are arranged and ordered around a raised central walkway that runs along the long axis of the site. At one end is a communications tower, shaped like a monumental tripod that soars 327 m into the air, creating a landmark for the site and the city. Next to the tower is a low slung, elliptical structure that houses the library, several auditoria and restaurants and is topped by the giant globe of the planetarium. The museum element is contained in a long ribbed building that runs along the river's edge to the north of the site, offering a point of contact with nature. The main exhibition hall is a spatial tour de force, interspersed with a series of cantilevered galleries and enclosed by a spectacular, organically curving roof.

1
Cross section through the museum.

2
Roof plan of the museum.

3
Location plan.

4
View of the museum showing the main façade.

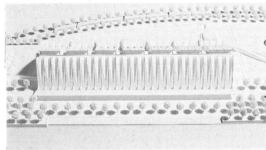

2

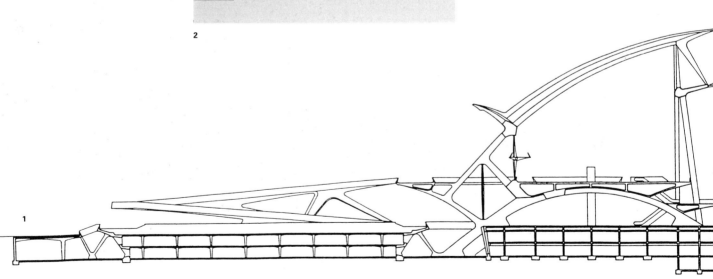

1

Science Museum, Valencia | **58**

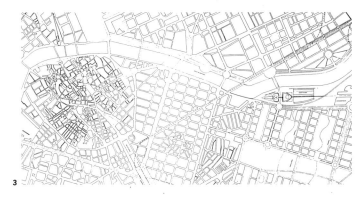

3

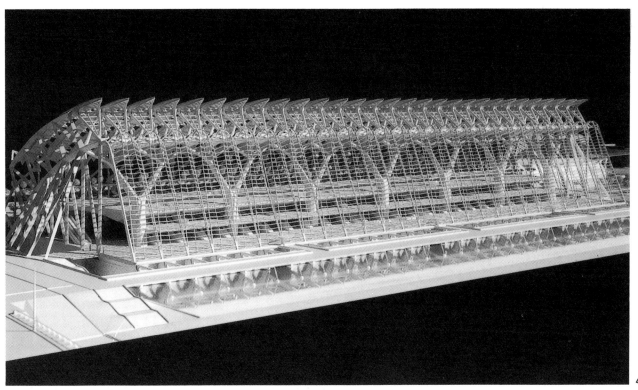

4

Science Museum, Valencia | 59

1
Part elevation of the planetarium.

2
Side view of the planetarium with the museum beyond.

3
Bird's eye view of the planetarium model.

4
A recent version of the communications tower model.

5
Two facets of the 1993 version of the communications tower.

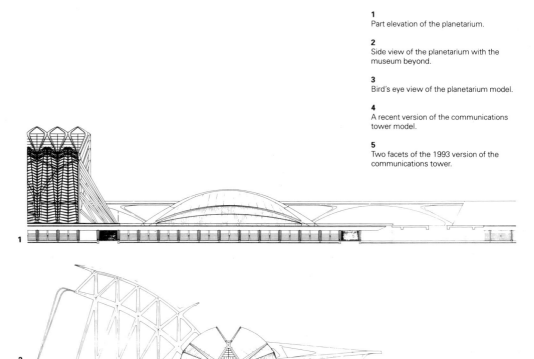

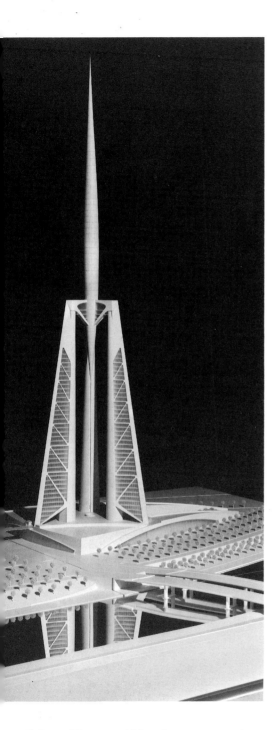

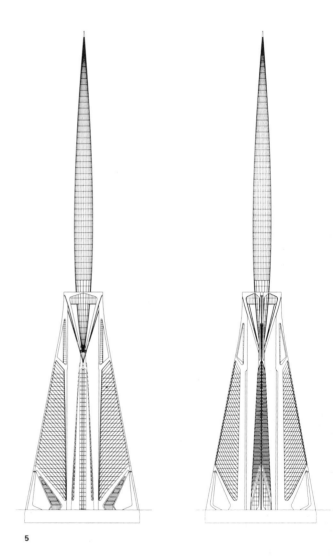

5

Science Museum, Valencia | 61

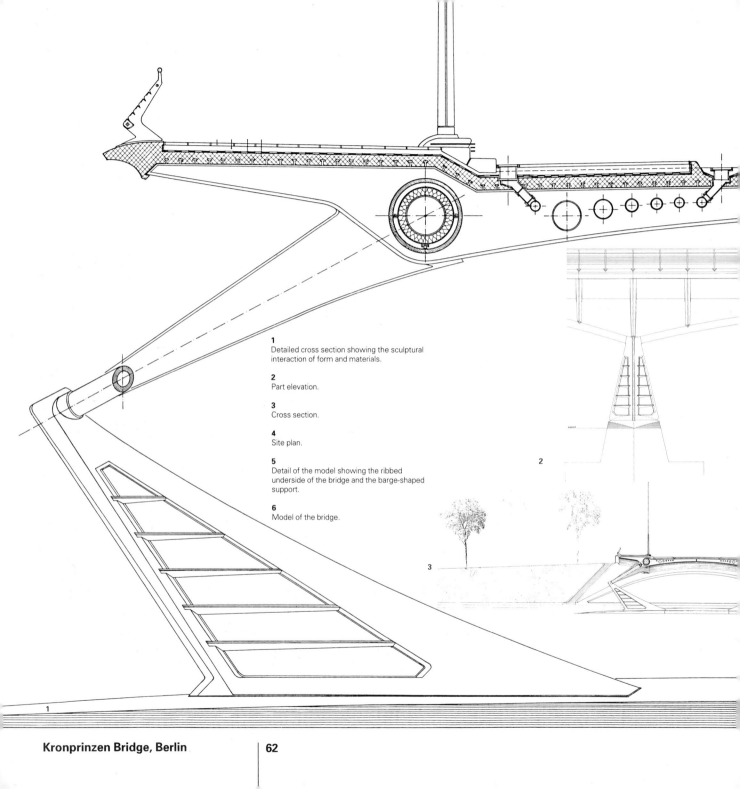

1
Detailed cross section showing the sculptural interaction of form and materials.

2
Part elevation.

3
Cross section.

4
Site plan.

5
Detail of the model showing the ribbed underside of the bridge and the barge-shaped support.

6
Model of the bridge.

Kronprinzen Bridge, Berlin | 62

The original Kronprinzen Bridge was built over the River Spree in Berlin between 1877–89. Like most Spree bridges it was based on Schinkel's Schloss Bridge and took the form of a triple steel arch supported by a series of masonry piers. The bridge was demolished in 1972 to prevent escape attempts from East to West Berlin. Since reunification, the area north of the Reichstag has become focus of intense redevelopment and in 1991 a competition was held to design a new bridge.

The competition was won by Santiago Calatrava and the winning design is now under construction. The new structure takes its cue from the traditional Spree bridges, with a single steel arch supported on two steel piers close to the river banks on the site of the original bridge. Appropriately, the piers are shaped like a pair of river barges. The deck is split into separate levels for cars, bicycles and pedestrians, with stairs at each end leading down to the riverbank. The lightness and delicacy of the structure imparts a modern dignity to its surroundings.

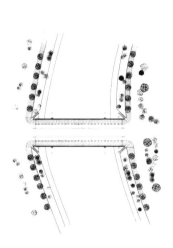

4

5

6

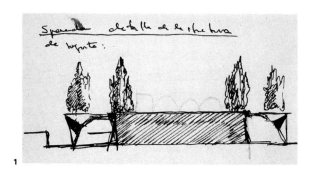

1
Sketch for revised version.

2
Cross section showing one of the two office buildings at one end. The network of tree-like canopy supports has a delicate organic quality.

3
Model of the station in context.

As part of Berlin's redevelopment drive following reunification, an international competition was held for the design of a major station in Spandau, in the north east corner of the city. The brief also included the provision of a significant element of commercial space. Calatrava's winning design involved suspending the main station structure between two rectangular office blocks, with the tracks actually running on a bridge through the buildings. These two office blocks define the outer edges of one end of a landscaped public park. Access to the platforms is via a bank of escalators. The glazed canopy structure over the platforms takes its cue from the trees in the park, with a network of intricate, organic, decidedly tree-like supports. This project is particularly interesting, because instead of a single, big structural statement, as might traditionally be expected in such a situation, Calatrava has opted for a relatively small gesture, repeated and interlinked, to form a complex, yet delicately homogenous whole.

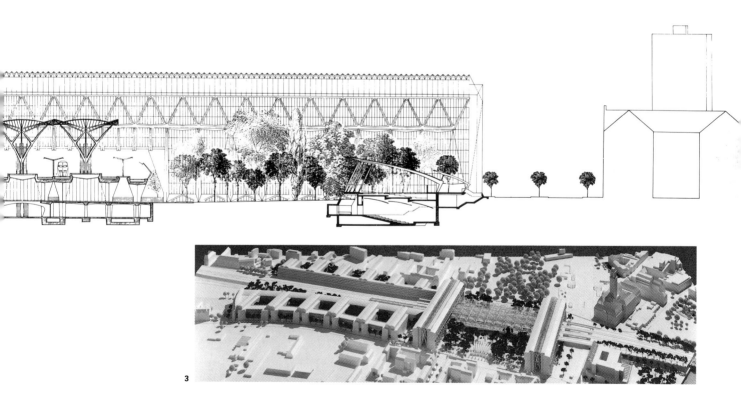

3

Spandau Railway Station, Berlin | **65**

Kuwaiti Pavilion, Seville 1991 - 92

The Government of Kuwait commissioned Santiago Calatrava to design its national pavilion for Expo '92, held in Seville. Although the Kuwaiti pavilion was one of the more modestly scaled structures among the 100 or so pavilions on the sprawling Expo site, it was certainly one of the most distinctive. The pavilion's exhibition and refreshment facilities were buried below ground in a shallow arched basement chamber. Above ground the arch read as a stepped plinth leading to a gently curving platform, covered with translucent panels. At night the platform glowed as light percolated through from the illuminated chamber below. However, the main structural tour de force was the set of spectacular hydraulic ribs that defined and enclosed the platform. The 17 concrete ribs were arranged in two rows (of 9 and 8), each pivoting on a thick tubular support rail that was in turn threaded through a series of tapering, inclined bases. The scimitar-shaped ribs were controlled by a system of hydraulics and could be manoeuvred from a 45° resting position up to 90°. The overall effect was quite stunning, like some huge prehistoric skeleton. The Kuwaiti Pavilion was the third in a series of kinetically oriented projects that began with the Swissbau '89 exhibition pavilion and continued with a proposed floating platform on Lake Lucerne to mark 700 years of Swiss democracy in 1989.

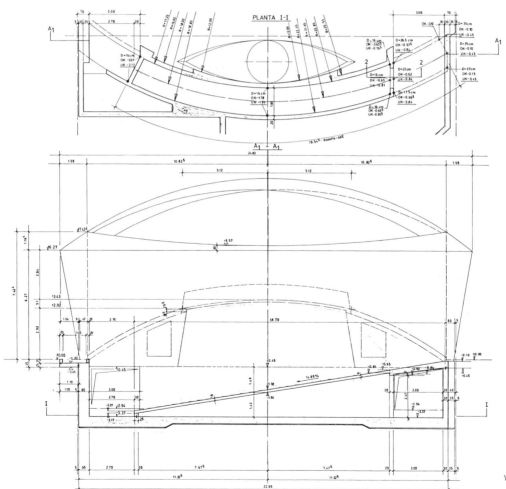

Working drawings.

1
The Kuwaiti Pavilion was a dynamic landmark among the scores of structures on the Expo site.

2
The giant ribs resemble a prehistoric skeleton.

3
The pavilion at night, with its glowing floor and the ribs arranged in a triumphal arch.

4
The ribs could be individually angled to create different configurations.
Previous page – detail of the surprisingly delicate timber rib structure.

1

Kuwaiti Pavilion, Seville

This proposal for a new concert hall in the Tenerife city of Santa Cruz is located on the city waterfront in the redeveloped harbour area. The idea behind the proposal was to create a new cultural and urban landmark for the city. The building consists of two auditoria, a main hall capable of housing 2,000 spectators and a smaller subsidiary space with a capacity of 400. The highly adaptable stage in the main hall can be rotated by 360° and enlarged according to requirements. The two auditoria are housed in a spectacular free-form structure, based on the interaction of conical and cylindrical volumes resting on a raised base. These are dominated by the gigantic curving prow of the main roof, which fully exploits the sculptural possibilities of thin-shelled concrete roof forms. The precisely curved shape resembles a huge bird poised in flight, one of Calatrava's favourite visual metaphors used at the Lyon TGV terminal and Sondica airport. In this respect, the Tenerife concert hall appears almost as one of his sculptures.

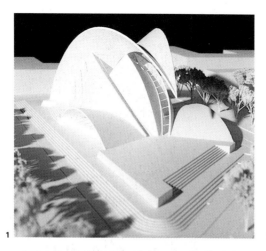

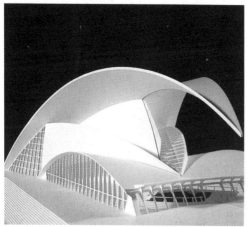

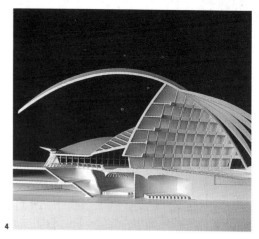

Previous page – model of the proposed concert hall with its dominant curved roof like a bird in flight.

1, 2
Model of the first scheme. The distinctive form of the roof structure is clearly evident at this stage.

3, 4
Model of the second stage, showing how sculptural interaction of the volumes has been progressively refined.

1

The East London River Crossing lies to the east of the Royal Docks and London City Airport. It carries the busy North Circular orbital road across the River Thames. Calatrava's elegant proposal was developed as a possible alternative to the original box girder structure. The design consists of a single tied arch sprung off triangular bases on each side of the river, forming a graceful continuous span from bank to bank. The central portion is 240 m long, the total arch 450 m and the overall structure 630 m. The design uses steel throughout, with the two supports in concrete. For various reasons the proposal was rejected, thus further impoverishing the beleaguered London skyline.

2

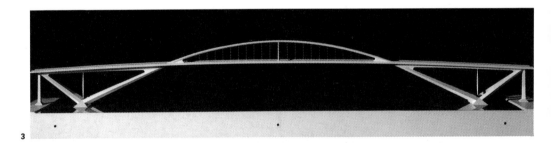

3

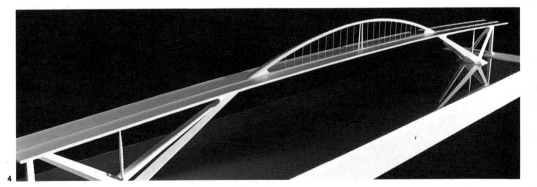

1
Sketch of the proposed bridge.

2
Elevation. The structure traverses the River Thames in one elegant span.

3, 4
Model of the bridge. The arch penetrates the deck, separating the traffic lanes.

Opposite page – photomontage of the bridge in context. The east London skyline has been deprived of a potentially enriching feature.

4

Cross section through dome.

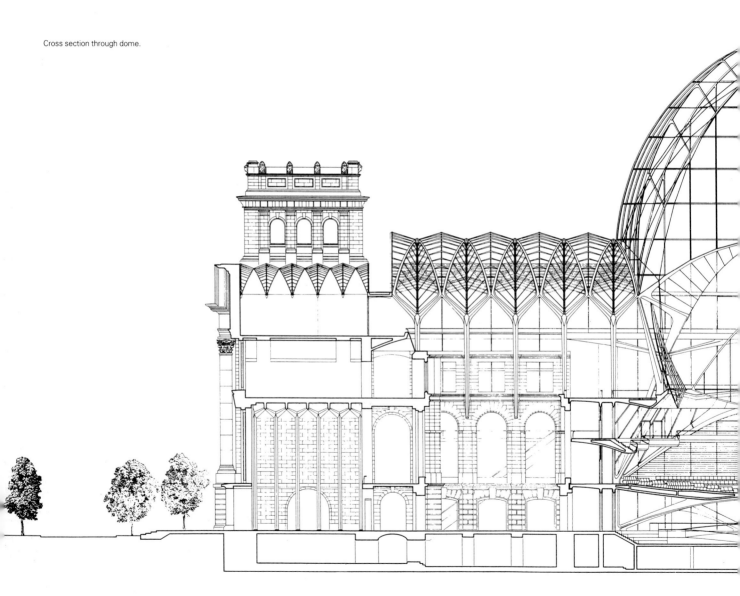

Reichstag, Berlin

Reichstag Conversion, Berlin 1992

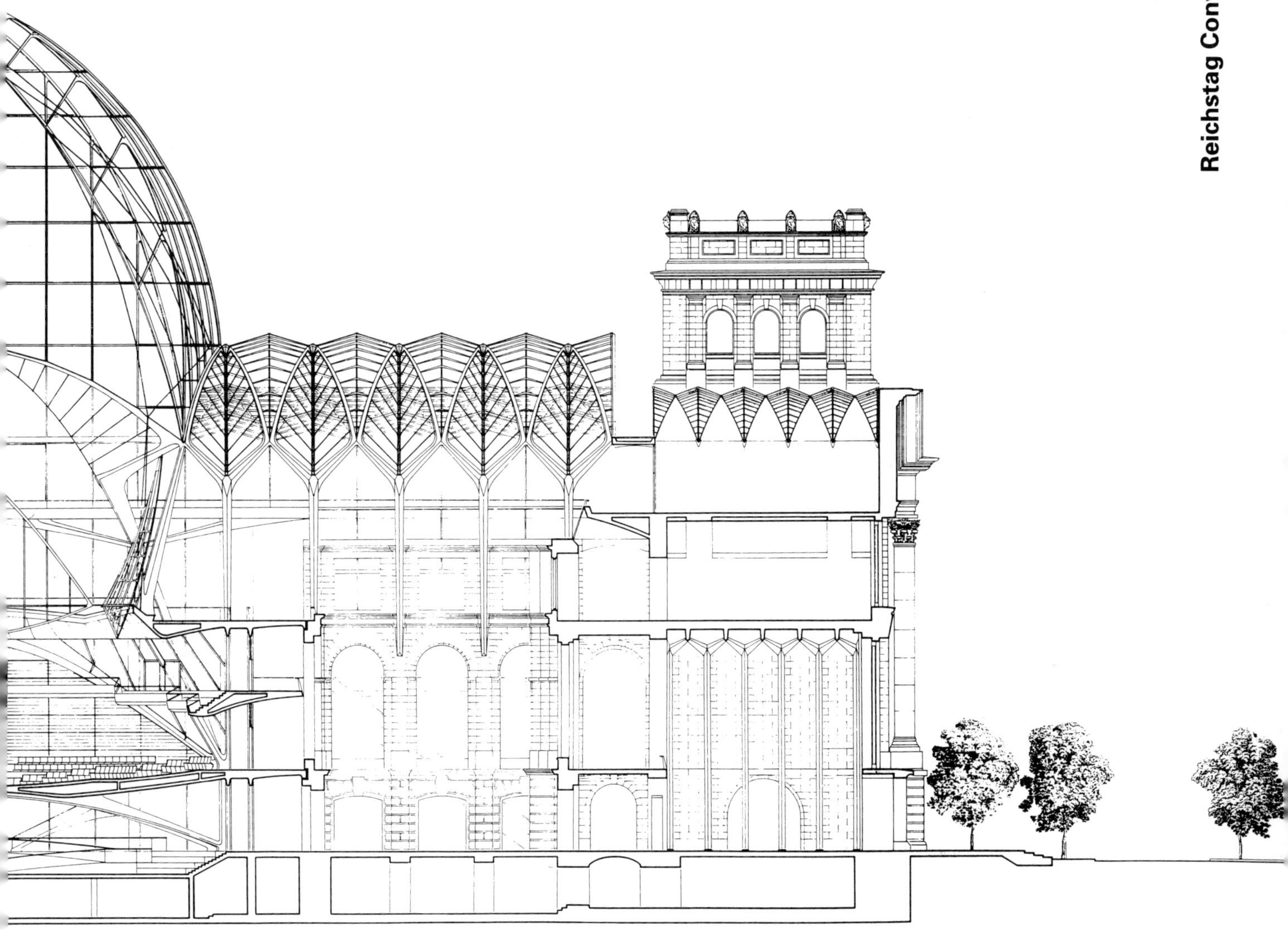

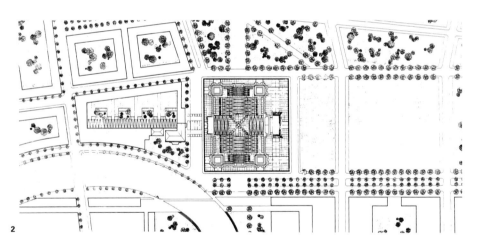

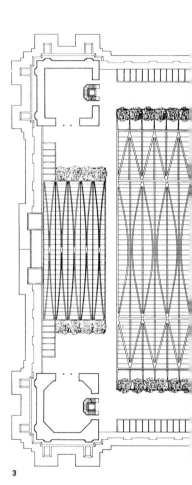

1
The Reichstag, front façade.

2
Site plan.

3
Roof plan.

4
Model looking towards the dome.

Reichstag, Berlin | 76

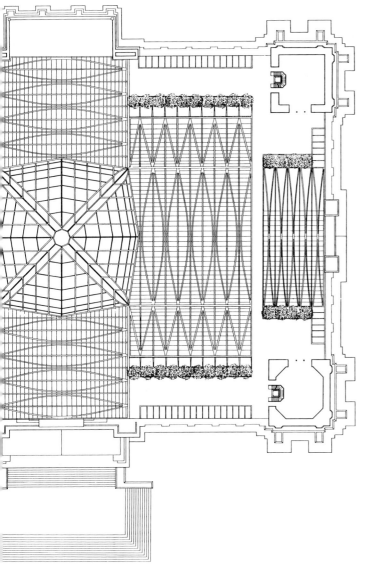

In 1991 Germany's old seat of government, the Reichstag in Berlin, was earmarked as the new Bundestag. The proposed conversion was opened up to international competition and in March 1993 Santiago Calatrava was awarded one of the three first prizes. Calatrava's scheme was the most respectful of the three quite disparate approaches to the old building, which was originally designed by Paul Wallot in 1883. Calatrava retained the idea of a central dome, but in glass and imbued with lightness and transparency. Four glazed inner courts, used for meeting rooms, allow light to penetrate deep into the heart of the well ordered new spaces.

4

Reichstag, Berlin | 77

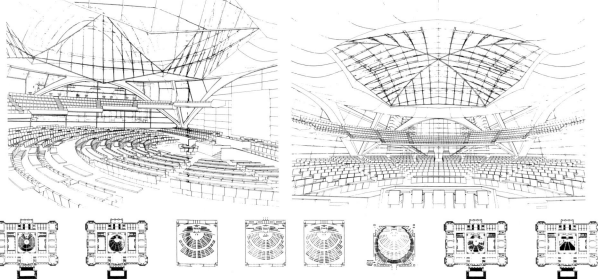

Reichstag, Berlin

1
Rear elevation of the Reichstag building with the Presidential Palace.

2
Two sketches of the plenary chamber, with floor plans below.

3
Cut-away axonometric showing the plenary chamber.

The Reichstag's external appearance and its surroundings remained largely unaltered. Parliamentary rooms were placed behind the Presidential Palace and connected to the Reichstag by underground routes. The plenary chamber lies under the dome with its movable glass roof which permits light to enter from above. Unfortunately this brilliantly sensitive solution, which during the second stage was developed into a highly sophisticated design, will never see the light of day.

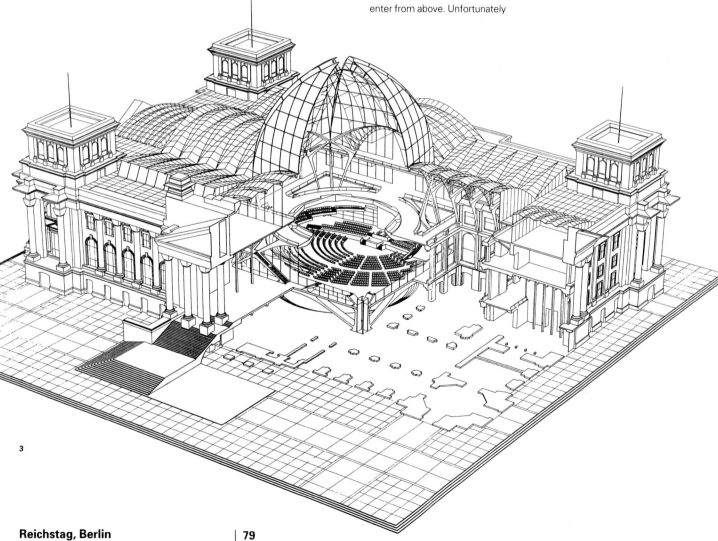

3

Reichstag, Berlin | 79

1
Longitudinal section.

2
Section through the crossing.

3
South elevation.

4
Section through the nave.

5
A recent version of the new model showing
the tower feature.

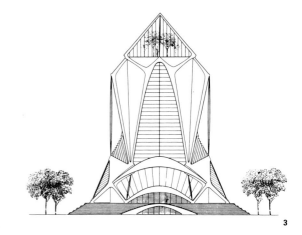

3

1

2

Calatrava's competition design for a 'Bioshelter' and a new south transept for Heins and Lafarge's great unfinished neo-Gothic cathedral on the upper west side of New York was received with enthusiasm by the jury. Philip Johnson referred to its organically inspired design as the only entry (there were 65) that put modern forms into a Gothic structure. Throughout the body of the church and supported on organically-shaped structural members of steel and stone the architect has created a high level eco-garden environment in the attic beneath a totally glazed roof. As in a rain forest, trees, hanging vines and other plants will help cool the interior of this biologically developed scheme. The public will be allowed to walk through these heavenly strata at a height of approximately 55 m above the nave floor. Funds are currently being sought by the Cathedral authorities to carry out the project which, as the latest model shows, now boasts a distinctive central spire.

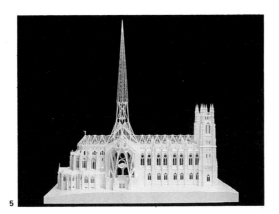

5

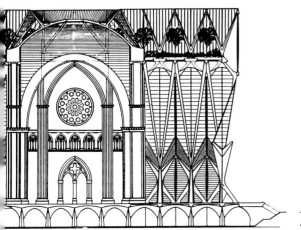

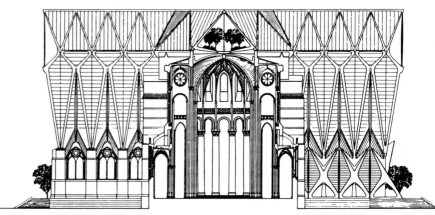

4

St. John the Divine, New York | 81

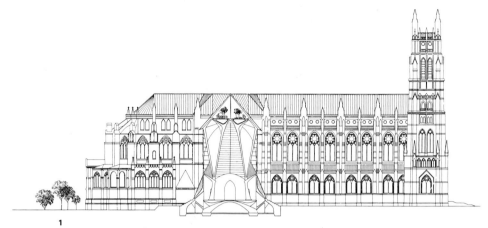

1

1
Cross section through the south transept.

2
Bioshelter plan at level ±38.70.

3
Ground floor level plan ±0.00.

4
Model showing the organically inspired
columnar construction and the tower.

5
Cross section through the north transept.

6
Cross section through the model.

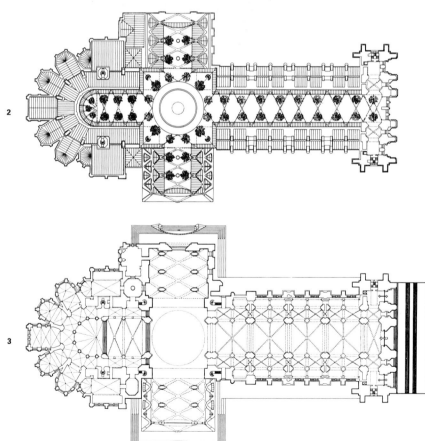

2

3

4

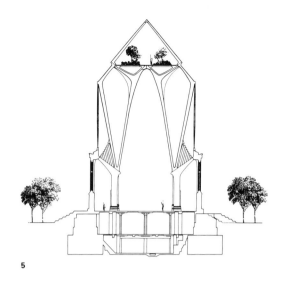

5

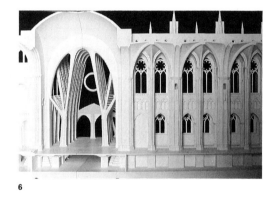

6

St. John the Divine, New York | 83

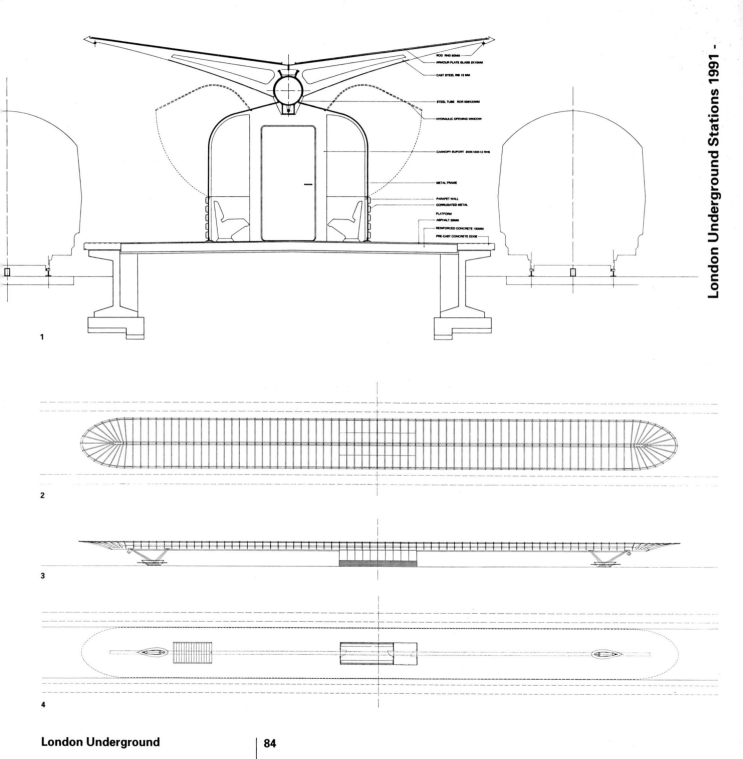

ROD RHD 60MM
ARMOUR PLATE GLASS 2X10MM
CAST STEEL RIB 12 MM

STEEL TUBE ROR 500X20MM

HYDRAULIC OPENING WINDOW

CANOPY SUPORT 200X150X12 RHS

METAL FRAME

PARAPET WALL
CORRUGATED METAL
PLATFORM
ASPHALT 20MM
REINFORCED CONCRETE 150MM
PRE-CAST CONCRETE EDGE

1

2

3

4

1
Modular station, cross section through
waiting room.

2
Roof plan.

5

3
Elevation.

4
Modular station platform plan.

5
Single-sided station, cross section through
waiting room.

6
Elevation.

7
Single-sided station platform plan.

8
Detail of the canopy support and bench.

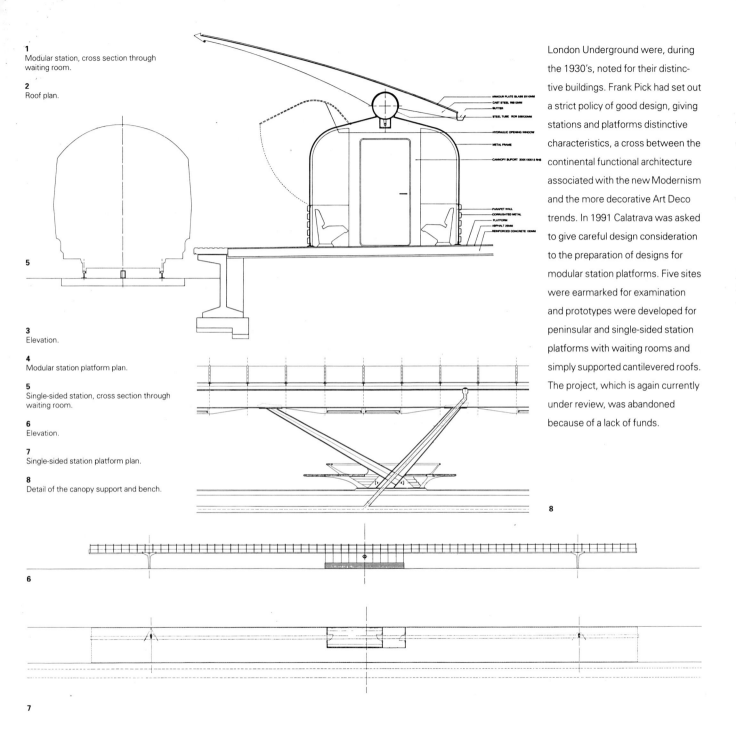

London Underground were, during
the 1930's, noted for their distinctive buildings. Frank Pick had set out
a strict policy of good design, giving
stations and platforms distinctive
characteristics, a cross between the
continental functional architecture
associated with the new Modernism
and the more decorative Art Deco
trends. In 1991 Calatrava was asked
to give careful design consideration
to the preparation of designs for
modular station platforms. Five sites
were earmarked for examination
and prototypes were developed for
peninsular and single-sided station
platforms with waiting rooms and
simply supported cantilevered roofs.
The project, which is again currently
under review, was abandoned
because of a lack of funds.

8

6

7

1, 2
Sketches of the bridge by Calatrava.

3
Model of the bridge with the pylon support in
Salford on the right.

1

2

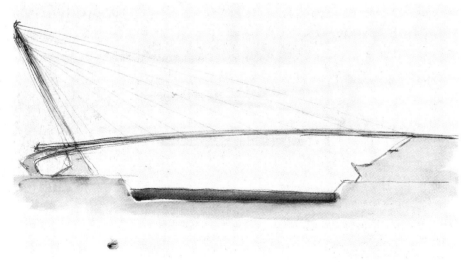

3

Spanning the 36 m wide River Irwell, the new Trinity Bridge provides a pedestrian link between Salford and Manchester. The bridge springs from the Salford side of the river, reaching over towards Manchester from an elegant, highly visible single balanced steel pylon support.

Stainless steel tension stay cables carry the bridge span and its two ramp entries on the Salford side. The design achieves a symmetrical equilibrium. A single point of access on the Manchester side filters pedestrians through to a new car park and an extensive redevelopment of a largley underused site on the Salford side of the river. The bridge spans approximately 60 m and the slender steel pylon reaches a height of 41 m, including its concrete base. The pylon is tilted at an angle of roughly 62°. All the light fittings for the bridge and the services are integrated into the design and are covered with strong grids to deter vandalism.

The clients for the project are the City of Salford; associated architects are Dennis Sharp Architects, London; consulting engineers: Buro Happold, Leeds.

1
Plan view of preliminary project.

2
Model: Salford side to the left.

3
Entry to pedestrian routes via stairs and ramp at Salford.

4
Working drawings and details of the bridge, first stage scheme, 1993.

5
Detail section through bridge.

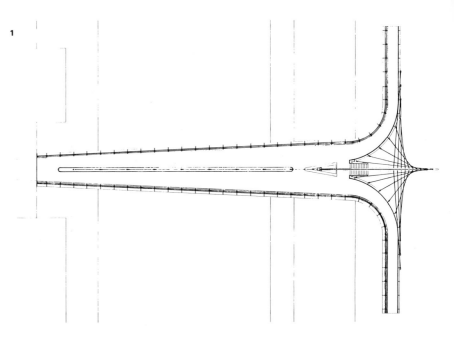

1

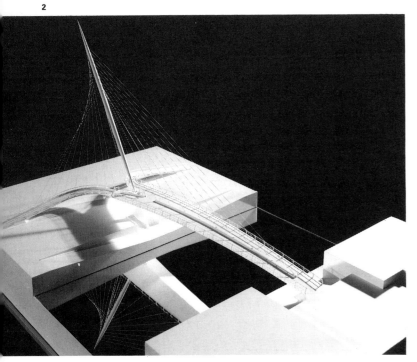

2

3

Trinity Bridge, Salford | 88

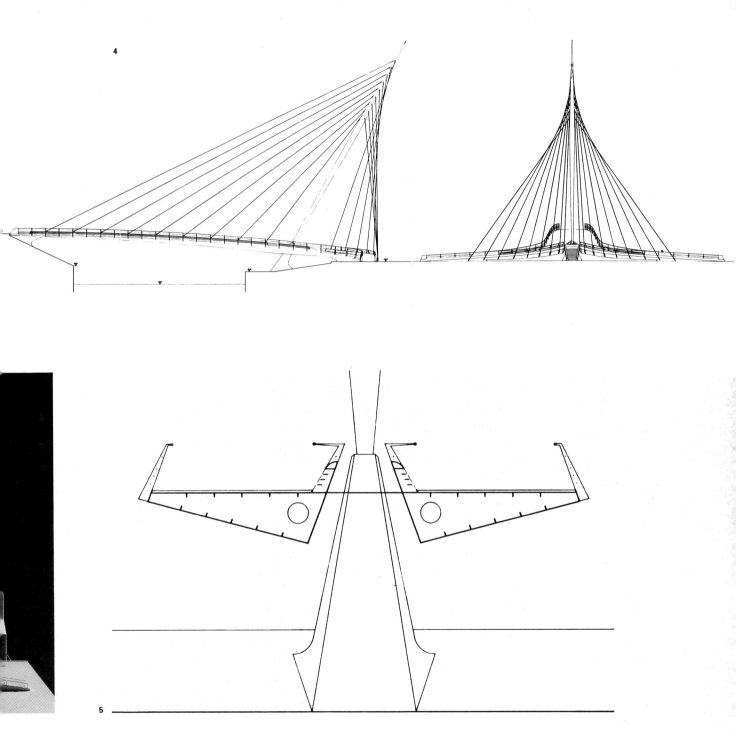

4

5

Trinity Bridge, Salford | 89

Underpass, Stadelhofen Railway Station, Zürich.

Selection of Works, Bibliography

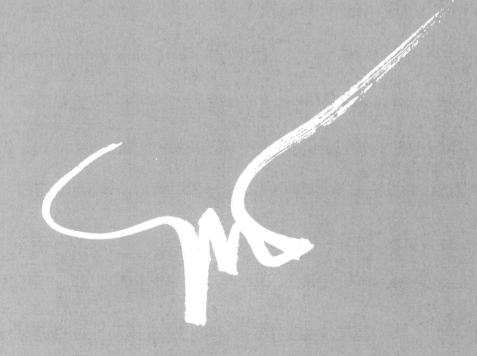

**Santiago Calatrava
Selection of Works**

1981 Züspa Exhibition Hall
Zürich, Switzerland (Project)
Competition with M. Spühler

1982 Letten Bridge
Zürich, Switzerland (Project)
Competition with Marbach &
Ruegg

City Library
Thun, Switzerland (Project)
Competition with Marbach &
Ruegg

Rhine Bridge
Diepoldsau, Switzerland (Project)
Competition with Weser and
Wolfensberger

1983 Jakem Steelwarehouse
Münchwilen, Switzerland (1983–84)

Ernstings Warehouse (Facades)
Coesfeld, Germany (1983–85)
Competition with Reichlin &
Reinhard

Stadelhofen Railway Station
Zürich, Switzerland (1983–90)
Competition with A. Amsler and
W. Ruegger

Bus Stop Shelter
St. Gallen, Switzerland (1983–85)

Post Office Dispatch (Canopy)
Lucerne, Switzerland (1983–85)

1984 Wohlen High School (4 roofs)
Wohlen, Switzerland (1984–88)
With Burkard, Meyer and Steiger

Lucerne Station Hall
Lucerne, Switzerland (1984–89)
With Ammann and Baumann

Bärenmatte Community Centre
Suhr, Switzerland (1984-88)

De Sede Mobile Pavilion
Zürich, Switzerland (1984)

1985 Residenz Neugebaeude Bridge
Salzburg, Austria (Project)
Competition

1987 Alamillo Bridge
Seville, Spain (1987–92)

Oudry-Mesly Bridge
Cretail/Paris, France (1987–88)

BCE Place: Galleria & Heritage
Square
Toronto, Canada (1987–92)

Bach de Roda

1985 Caballeros Bridge
Lerida, Spain (Project)
Competition

Bach de Roda Bridge
Barcelona, Spain (1985–87)

Station Square Lucerne
(2 bus shelters) Lucerne,
Switzerland (Project)
Competition

9 de Octubre Bridge
Valencia, Spain (1986–90)

Blackbox Television Studio
Zürich, Switzerland (1986–87)

Tabourettli Theatre
Basle, Switzerland (1986–87)

Stadelhofen

1987 Underground Station Bilbao
Bilbao, Spain
(Project) Competition

Housing Estate Buchen
Würenlingen, Switzerland (1987–)

1988 Lusitania Bridge
Merida, Spain (1988–90)

Wettstein Bridge
Basle, Switzerland (Project)

Gentil Bridge
Paris, France (Project)
Competition

Pré Babel Sport Centre
Geneva, Switzerland (Project)

1989 Montjuïc Communications Tower
Barcelona, Spain (1989–92)

Swissbau Pavilion
Basle, Switzerland (1989)

Bauschänzli Restaurant
Zürich, Switzerland (Project)

Bus Stop Shelter
St. Gallen, Switzerland (Project)

Lyon Airport Railway Station
Lyon-Satolas (1989–94)
Competition

Floating Pavilion
Lake at Lucerne, Switzerland
(Project)

Miraflores Bridge
Cordoba, Spain (Project)

Puerto Bridge
Ondarroa, Spain (Project)

La Devesa Bridge
Ripoll, Spain (1989–91)

1990 Uribitarte Bridge
Bilbao, Spain (Project)

Spitalfields Gallery
London, England (Project)

East London River Crossing
London, England (Project)

Sondica Airport
Bilbao, Spain (Project)

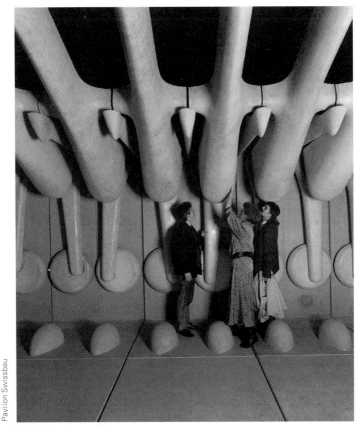

Pavilion Swissbau

1991 Tenerife Concert Hall
Santa Cruz, Spain (Project)

Television Tower Valencia
Valencia, Spain (Project)
Competition

Kuwait Pavilion Expo '92
Seville, Spain (Project)

Science Museum
Valencia, Spain (Project)
Competition

Alameda Metro Station
Valencia, Spain (Project)
Competition

Médoc Bridge
Bordeaux, France (Project)
Competition

1991 Cathedral of St. John the Divine
New York, USA (Project)
Competition

Kronprinzen Bridge
Berlin, Germany (1991–95)
Competition

Spandau Railway Station
Berlin, Germany (Project)
Competition

1992 Jahn Sport Complex
Berlin, Germany (Project)
Competition

Solferino Bridge
Paris, France (Project)
Competition

London Underground Modular
Station
London, England (Project)

Exhibition Hall, Santa Cruz
Tenerife, Spain (Project)
Competition

1993 Reichstag Competition
Berlin, Germany
Shared first prize

Oresund Bridge
Denmark–Sweden
Competition entry

Trinity Bridge
Salford, UK

Kunsthalle NY
New York, USA

Ile Falcon Motorway Bridge
Sion, Switzerland

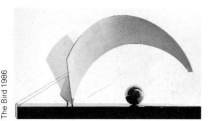

The Bird 1986

28 July 1951
Santiago Calatrava Valls
born in Benimamet,
Valencia, Spain.

1968–69
Schooling In Valencia. Attends art school

1969–74
Studies architecture at the 'Escuela Technica Superior de Arquitectura de Valencia' qualifying as an architect. Post graduate course in urbanism.

1975–79
Studies civil engineering at the Swiss Federal Institute of Technology, ETH Zürich.

1979–81
Doctorate of Technical Science of the ETH. Phd. thesis: On the Foldability of Space Frames.

Assistant in the Institute for Building Statics and Construction and in the Institute for Aerodynamics and Lightweight Construction at the ETH Zürich.

1981
Architecture and engineering practice established in Zürich

1987
Member of the BSA (Union of Swiss Architects)

'Auguste Perret UIA' Prize (Union Internationale d'Architectes), Paris

Member of the 'International Academy of Architecture'

1988
Art prize of the city of Barcelona for the Bach de Roda Bridge

'Premie de la Asociacion de la prensa', Award of the Press Association, Valencia

IABSE Award (International Association for Bridge and Structural Engineering)

FAD Prize, (Formento de las Artes y el Diseño), Spain

Fritz Schumacher Prize for 'Urbanism, Architecture and Engineering' Hamburg, Germany

Fazlur Rahman Khan International Fellowship for Architecture and Engineering

1989
Honorary Member of BDA (Union of German Architects)

Second Architectural and Engineering practice established in Paris

1990
'Medaille d'Argent de la Recherche et de la Technique', (Academie d'Architecture Foundation 1970) Paris

1991
European 'Glulam Award'. (Glued Laminated Timber Construction) Munich

'Award for good buildings 1991' Zürich, for Stadelhofen Railway Station

1992
Member at the 'Real Academia de Bellas Artes de San Carlos', Valencia

Brunel Award for Stadelhofen Railway Station

Gold Medal of the Institution of Structural Engineers, London

1993
Hon. Fellow, Royal Institute of British Architects

Doctor Honoris Causa, University of Valencia

The City of Toronto Urban Design Awards, Award of excellence for the BCE Place Galleria

Books and Monographs

Weber, Jamileh (Ed);
Santiago Calatrava,
Edition Jamileh Weber
Zürich 1986,
Exhibition catalogue

Nicolin, Pierluigi (Ed);
Il folle volo/The daring flight,
Lotus Documents,
Milan 1987

Blaser, Werner (Ed);
Santiago Calatrava:
Engineering-Architecture,
Birkhäuser Verlag,
Basel 1987

Levene, Richard C./Cecilia,
Fernando Marquez (Ed);
Monografia Santiago Calatrava,
el Croquis 38/1992,
Madrid 1989

Klein B./Frampton K. *et al*;
Ein Bahnhof – Un Gare,
Archithese,
Zürich 1990

Stahl-Informations-Zentrum/
Schweizerische Zentralstelle für
Stahlbauten (Ed);
Theater Tabourettli Basel,
Stahl und Form,
Munich 1991

Calatrava, Santiago;
Dynamic Equilibrium/
Recent Projects,
Artemis Verlag 1992

Harbison, Robert;
Creatures from the Mind of
the Engineer –
The Architecture
of Santiago Calatrava,
Artemis Verlag 1992

Frampton K. *et al*;
Calatrava Bridges
Zürich, London,
Artemis 1993

Magazine Articles

Reinhart, Fabio;
Declaro a favore di Santiago
Calatrava,
Quaderns 160,
Barcelona 1/1984, p38–40

Oechslin, Werner;
Technology's Representation,
Lotus International, 1/1985, p7

Ortelli, Luca;
The Art of Science,
Lotus International, 1/1985 p28–38

Nolli, Aldo
Bridges and Canopies,
Lotus International,
3/1985, p92–114

Vayssiere, Bruno Henry;
Santiago Calatrava,
Crée No.208 10/1985, p108

Rastorfer, Darl;
The Structural Art of Santiago
Calatrava,
Architectural Record, (USA)
8/1986, p130–139

Quetglas, Jose;
Technology is the Base of Lyricism,
A & U (Architecture & Urbanism)
No. 192 9/86, p81–112

Lucan, Jacques;
Santiago Calatrava,
AMC No16 6/87, p4–23

Van Berkel, and Bos, Caroline;
Flights of Science – the Work of
Santiago Calatrava,
AA Files no.16 Autumn 1987

Buchanan, Peter;
Calatrava – Expressive Engineering,
Architectural Review, 9/1987, p50–61

Nolli, Aldo;
Trail Sign – Santiago Calatrava:
Bridge in Barcelona,
Lotus International No.56 4/1987, p62–73

Selected bibliography in date order

De Carli, Giulio;
Cabaret Tabourettli Basilea,
Domus No.679, 9/1988, p52–61

Wyss, Alfred;
**The Renovation of the Spalenhof –
A Cabaret-theater by Santiago
Calatrava in Basle,**
Lotus International No.58 2/1988,
p106–117

Peters, Tom F.;
Crossing Boundaries,
Progressive Architecture, 4/89,
p98–103

Koenig, Giovanni Klaus;
My Aspiration: Santiago Calatrava,
A & U (Architecture & Urbanism)
No.224 5/89, p59–121

Baracco, Mauro;
Milano 89, Lampada Montjuïc,
Domus No.708, 9/1989, p125–127

Buchanan, Peter;
Planes, Trains & Automobiles,
Architectural Review, 12/1989,
p50–53

Calatrava, Santiago;
**The Synthetic Power of Games and
Metaphor,**
Transcript of a lecture held at the
Guggenheim Museum, New York, April,
1989

Lemoine, Bertrand;
Forces in Play as Sculptures,
L'Architecture d'aujourd'hui No.267
2/1990, p90–113

Sutherland, James;
One Man Orchestra,
New Builder No.32 5/1990,
p22–23

Metz, Tracy;
Structural Dynamics.
Architectural Record No. 10, 10/1990,
p50–61

Binney, Marcus;
Making Steel Sing for a Living,
The European, Zürich 11/1990,
p6–7

Bridging the Gap
Building Arts Forum, New York, 1990

Buchanan, Peter;
**Artist & Baumeister –
Santiago Calatrava,**
Architectural Review, 1/1991, p45ff

Calatrava/Amsler/Rüegger,
Stadelhofen Train Station, Zürich,
Global Architecture Document No.28,
1991, p45–59

Pousse, Jean-François
**'Haute Tension – Station de
Stadelhofen, Zurich, Suisse,**
Techniques & Architecture, 2/1991,
p106–115

Calatrava, Santiago;
Station Lyon-Satolas, France,
GA Document No.29 4/1991, p14–17

Stroud, Andrew;
Interview with S. Calatrava
Concrete Quarterly, Spring 1991,
p22–25

Zardini, Mirko;
**La Stazione Stadelhofen a Zurigo di
Santiago Calatrava,**
Lotus 69, 8/1991, p6–32

Frampton, Kenneth;
Calatrava at Stadelhofen,
A & U (Architecture & Urbanism) No.251,
8/1991, p48–79

Metz, Tracy;
Express Track,
Architectural Record, 8/1991, p84–89

Candela, Felix;
Calatrava's Graceful Shapes,
World Architecture No.13, 1991,
p46–57

Pawley, Martin;
The Engineer Unchained,
Blueprint No.85, 3/1992, p24

Tischhauser, Anthony;
Tree of Life,
Architectural Review No. 1142, 4/1992,
p34–37

Selected Exhibitions

1985
Jamileh Weber Gallery, Zürich
Sculptures

1985–86
Fundacio Joan Miró, Barcelona
Sculptures and architecture

1987
Triennale di Milano

Museum of Architecture, Basle

1988
Berowergut Basle
Sculptures, drawings, architecture

1989
1st Travelling Exhibition, New York,
St. Louis, Chicago, Los Angeles

1990–91
2nd Travelling Exhibition, Toronto.
Montreal, Helsinki

'Dynamics and Equilibrium', Museum of
Design, Zürich
Retrospective

1992
Nederlands Architectuur Instituut,
Rotterdam
Retrospective

RIBA, London
Retrospective

1993
'Structure and Expression', MOMA,
New York

La Llonja, Valencia
Retrospective

Danish Association of Architects,
Gammel Dok, Copenhagen

'Santiago Calatrava Bridges', Deutsches
Museum, Munich

SC = Santiago Calatrava **Bold page numbers** indicate main entrie